COMPOSTING
THE GARDEN GOLD

[6-IN-1] FROM WASTE TO WEALTH: BOOSTING SOIL PRODUCTIVITY AND EMBRACING A GREENER LIFESTYLE

OLIVER THORNE

Photo credits: Depositphotos, Canva Pro, Shutterstock

ISBN eBook : 978-1-961963-31-3
ISBN Paperback : 978-1-961963-32-0

Contents

COMPOSTING IS NOT
JUST A PROCESS,
IT'S A MINDSET –
A COMMITMENT TO
NURTURING OUR
ENVIRONMENT, ONE
DECOMPOSED SCRAP
AT A TIME.

INTRODUCTION

In the beginning, there was dirt. It was under our fingernails, smudged on our jeans, nestled in the crevices of our garden boots. But for those of us who weren't already part of the green-thumbed club, it was just dirt. It held no particular fascination or mystery, no allure or promise. That is, until one day when it became much more than that.

The story begins when I was a child, spending the balmy summer afternoons playing in my grandmother's garden. She would carefully dig her hands into the soft, damp soil, revealing a world of earthworms, decomposed leaves, and fragments of yesterday's kitchen waste. It was a thriving, bustling universe right beneath our feet, full of life and activity. "It is Garden Gold," she said. I can still hear her quiet chuckle as if she had just told herself a joke that only she would get.

As a child, I didn't fully grasp the concept. It was just the dirt beneath the roses, the soil that stained my hands, and the substance that held the key to my grandmother's inexplicably large tomatoes. Only much later, when the mantle of the garden was passed onto me, I understood the profound truth behind her words. It was compost, the decomposed remnants of once-living things, that was the lifeblood of her garden. It was the secret to her lush green leaves, colorful flowers, and juicy vegetables.

And now, my friends, I want to share that secret with you. Welcome to "Composting: The Garden Gold." This book is your definitive guide to composting, a practice as old as agriculture itself yet novel and exciting to many of us in the modern world.

Composting is much more than just a way to reduce household waste, though that's a significant part of its appeal. It is a pathway to healthier soil, better produce, and a more sustainable lifestyle. It's about taking responsibility for our waste, transforming what was once discarded into something useful, valuable, and, dare I say, even miraculous.

The Power and Potential of Composting

Composting is a marvelous process of transformation. It's proof that Mother Nature can constantly renew herself through recycling and rebirth. It's about taking waste – the peels of your morning banana, the spent coffee grounds, the withered lettuce leaves – and turning it into black gold, a rich, nutritious, and fertile soil conditioner.

Composting is a gardener's best friend, a secret weapon in the fight against poor soil and disappointing harvests. This is where the magic happens. In the decomposition, the breakdown of organic material by microbes, fungi, and tiny creatures, we find the real value of compost. It strengthens the soil's structure, increases its ability to retain water, and infuses it with essential nutrients.

Why Composting Matters: For You, Your Garden, and the Planet

Composting matters because it's a tangible, practical way to address some of the most pressing issues of our time: waste management, soil degradation, and climate change. It's about taking small, sustainable steps at an individual level that can lead to significant change when multiplied by millions of people.

For you, it means reducing your household waste, saving money on fertilizer, and engaging in a rewarding and educational process. It means healthier plants, better produce, and improved soil for your garden. And for the planet, it means less waste ending up in landfills, where it generates methane, a potent greenhouse gas.

In this guide, we will explore the art and science of composting. We'll dive into the nitty-gritty details of what to compost, how to maintain a healthy compost pile, and how to use compost to benefit your garden.

We'll discuss different types of composting methods, from the traditional backyard compost pile to innovative indoor composting solutions. We'll delve into worm composting, also known as vermicomposting, and for those of you living in apartments or homes without a yard, don't worry! We'll provide solutions for you too.

Are you concerned about odors, pests, or the time commitment required for composting? We have answers to all your worries. Whether you're a busy city dweller, a suburban homeowner, or a rural homesteader, you'll be equipped with valuable tips and tricks to make composting an enjoyable and rewarding part of your life. You'll also find practical advice on troubleshooting common composting problems.

Along the way, we'll share stories and insights from composting enthusiasts around the world. These people have discovered the joy and satisfaction of turning waste into wealth and have seen firsthand the positive impact of composting on their gardens, wallets, and the planet. They're part of a growing community of green thumbs, waste warriors, and soil stewards who are changing the world, one compost pile at a time.

By the time you turn the final pages of this book, you'll have not only a deep understanding of composting but a newfound respect for the transformative power of nature. You'll have the knowledge and confidence to build your own compost pile and maybe even inspire others to do the same.

But most importantly, I hope this book will help you see the beauty and value in what others may consider waste. I hope it will inspire you to look at your kitchen scraps, yard trimmings, and fallen leaves in a new light. And who knows? Maybe, like me, you'll find yourself knee-deep in your compost pile one day, marveling at the wriggling earthworms and the rich, earthy smell of decomposition, and you'll understand why my grandmother called it "Garden Gold."

So, are you ready to begin our journey together? Let's roll up our sleeves, dig our hands into the soil, and discover the wealth that lies within our waste. Welcome to the world of composting. Here's to greener gardens, less waste, and a healthier planet. Let's get composting!

BOOK I

COMPOSTING 101

TRANSFORMING WASTE
INTO GARDEN TREASURE

There is magic in the compost pile. It's where the unwanted becomes precious, the discarded becomes cherished, and waste transforms into wealth. But to unlock this magic, we must first understand the hidden processes at play, the unseen actors in this grand drama of decomposition.

Composting isn't a one-size-fits-all endeavor, and you'll find many options to suit every circumstance. We will explore the various composting methods. This can help you pick the composting strategy that best fits your lifestyle and needs, from backyard heaps to worm bins and tumblers to Bokashi.

Get ready to dig into the secrets of the compost pile. Waste-to-wealth begins right here!

Understanding The Composting Process: From Waste To Nutrient-Rich Soil

COMPOST LIFE CYCLE

FOOD   SCARPS   COMPOST   FERTILIZER   GROW

Composting is a symphony of transformation, a wondrous biological process that turns kitchen scraps and yard waste into a nutrient-rich, garden-enhancing material. Mother Nature conducts this organic orchestra like a grand maestro, where decomposing vegetable peels and fallen leaves become a fertile symphony. The process unfolds as if by magic, but the truth is, it's grounded in biology, chemistry, and a dash of plain old patience. From the initial act of discarding a wilted flower or a potato peel into the compost bin to the final flourish of spreading rich, crumbly compost onto your garden bed, composting is a journey of rebirth and renewal. It's proof that everything in life goes through cycles and that even decay may bring new life.

Picture the journey of a banana peel. After you've savored the fruit, the peel finds a new home in your compost bin. What once was considered waste is now on a path to becoming a treasure. Once vibrant yellow, this peel starts to brown and soften, surrendering to nature's course. It's no longer just a banana peel but a banquet for a microscopic army.

Tiny decomposers start to nibble away, turning it into an array of nutrients. Over weeks, the peel disintegrates its original form, only a memory. The once distinguishable peel morphs into a part of the collective, contributing to the nutrient-rich humus that gardeners dream of. Though humble, its journey is a testament to the miraculous cycle of life, death, and rebirth in the heart of a compost pile.

The Symphony of Decomposition

In the grand orchestra of composting, every type of waste plays a distinct, valuable role. Much like a symphony's harmony results from the cooperation of different instruments, the efficiency and success of composting derive from the interplay of various waste materials. Their decomposition pace and manner hinge upon several factors such as structure, moisture content, and their provided balance of carbon and nitrogen.

Starting the performance, we have the virtuosos, the expected stars of the compost bin—fruit and vegetable scraps. With their soft, succulent structure, these materials are high in moisture and brimming with nutrients. These attributes cause them to break down relatively quickly, often within a couple of weeks. They can be seen as the sprinters in the decomposition race—fast, furious, and tremendously effective at kickstarting the composting process.

Accompanying our virtuosos, we have the leafy greens - think spinach or lettuce - along with coffee grounds. Their role in our composting symphony is similar to that of the percussion section in an orchestra. They set the rhythm for the compost pile's decomposition process. Like the fruit and vegetable scraps, they decompose rapidly. However, their unique contribution is a hefty dose of nitrogen, a nutrient that fuels the composting process. Also, they are a gourmet treat for composting worms if you have them in your pile, assisting in further accelerating the process.

In this performance, grass clippings play a versatile role, similar to a talented musician who can switch between different instruments. Fresh clippings, teeming with nitrogen, decompose rapidly, turning up the heat in your compost pile. But when dried out, their role changes. They transform into a carbon source, adopting a steadier, slower pace of decomposition. This flexibility allows them to contribute effectively to the composting process in multiple ways.

In our composting orchestra, eggshells would be the brass section. They don't play all the time, but when they do, their contribution is crucial. Due to their hard, calcified structure, eggshells take longer to decompose. However, their contribution to the compost is valuable, providing essential calcium for plant health. To help them along, crushing eggshells before adding them to the compost can speed up their decomposition.

Finally, we have the "browns" - the stalwart string section of our compost symphony. These materials, like dried leaves, straw, paper, or wood chips, are high in carbon and decompose more slowly due to their tougher, more rigid structure. While they might not break down as rapidly as other materials, their role in the compost pile is akin to the consistent, driving melodies provided by a symphony's string section. They're the marathon runners of composting, pacing themselves, offering structure, and balancing out the faster-decomposing "greens."

This decomposition concert demonstrates that composting is not a race against time. Instead, it's a thoughtful, deliberate process where each element has its own unique role. From sprinters that break down quickly to marathon runners that decompose over more extended periods, every component is vital. Nature's recycling efficiency is on full display, resulting in the production of a rich, crumbly compost that's a testament to the combined decomposition of all these components at varying rates.

Oxygen and Moisture in Composting

A successful composting operation is essentially a bustling eco-metropolis. This city thrives on the diligent work of its unsung heroes: the countless microorganisms tirelessly breaking down organic matter day and night. Like their human counterparts in bustling cities, these microscopic workers depend on two primary resources: oxygen and water. Understanding the role of these two vital elements can greatly enhance the success and efficiency of your composting efforts.

Let's begin by viewing your compost pile as a living, breathing entity. For the microorganisms, oxygen is like the fresh breeze that sweeps through an open window in a high-rise building. Oxygen fuels their metabolic processes, energizing them to break down organic materials faster and more effectively. Introducing air into the compost pile, known as aeration, is achieved by physically turning or stirring the pile with a pitchfork or a specialized compost aerator. A well-aerated compost pile is a thriving one, brimming with microbial activity.

Now, consider water. Just as humans need water for survival and efficient functioning, so do the microorganisms in your compost pile. Water plays a crucial role in composting, acting as the lifeblood that keeps this thriving ecosystem ticking. It helps regulate the overall temperature of the compost pile, facilitates the transportation of nutrients and enzymes, and enables the vital biological reactions that turn waste materials into nutrient-rich compost.

But as with any city, balance is key. You are the steward of this micro metropolis, and it falls on you to ensure the moisture content is right. A compost pile that's too dry slows down the decomposition process due to reduced microbial activity. Conversely, an excessively wet compost pile can become anaerobic or oxygen-deprived, leading to slower decomposition and, often, unpleasant odors.

Think of maintaining the right moisture balance, like wringing out a sponge. You've achieved the perfect balance if you squeeze a handful of compost and only a few drops of water come out. The compost should feel moist to the touch, but it shouldn't be drenched.

Remember, your compost pile is a living, breathing entity that thrives with the right balance of air and water.

The Finished Product: Recognizing Ready Compost

Unveiling a batch of finished compost is a moment of anticipation and triumph, akin to a sculptor revealing their masterpiece or a chef presenting their signature dish.

But how do you know when your compost is ready? Picture a material that looks like crumbled chocolate cake, rich, dark, and teeming with life. Isn't that quite a transformation from the banana peels and leaf piles you began with? Ready compost boasts an earthy smell, like a forest after a gentle rain. There's a certain satisfaction in breathing in this fragrance, knowing that you've had a hand in creating it.

If you sift this crumbly goodness through your fingers, you might find some eggshells or twigs that weren't quite ready to break down, but that's alright. If you add them back to a fresh pile, these will continue to decompose. The real test, however, comes when you mix this black gold into your garden soil. Plants will thrive, earthworms will wriggle joyfully, and your garden's productivity will skyrocket.

How to use compost in your garden

Think of compost as the secret sauce of your garden, a nutrient-packed elixir that can transform even the most lackluster of soils. But how can you best utilize this black gold? Here are some time-tested methods:

1. Soil Amendment: Like a skilled masseuse kneading tension away, incorporating compost into your garden soil loosens it up and improves its

structure. For clay soils, compost aids in breaking up compacted layers, enhancing their drainage capabilities. It acts like a sponge for sandy soils, retaining precious moisture and nutrients. Mix generous amounts of compost when preparing your garden beds for the planting season to boost your soil.

2. Mulch: A layer of compost spread around your plants is a protective shield, much like a snug blanket on a chilly winter's night. It helps maintain soil moisture, suppresses weed growth, and continuously feeds your plants with nutrients as it slowly decomposes. Picture your tomatoes, basil, and zucchinis basking in the comfort of a compost mulch!

3. Potting Mix Ingredient: For container gardening enthusiasts, compost is essential to any homemade potting mix. Blend it with coir, peat moss, perlite, or vermiculite to create a light, nutrient-rich mix that your potted plants will adore.

4. Compost Tea: Brew a nutrient-rich tea for your plants by steeping compost in water. This compost tea can be used to water plants, providing a gentle, continuous source of nutrients. It's like serving your plants a hearty, healthy soup, keeping them nourished and happy.

Each method harnesses the power of compost in different ways, nurturing not just your plants but the entire garden ecosystem.

Advantages of Composting

Environmental Impact

Composting offers numerous environmental benefits, making it good for your garden and the planet. Here's how:

1. Waste Reduction: A large percentage of household waste is organic material, much of which can be composted. Composting your kitchen scraps, yard waste, and

other compostable materials reduces the waste in landfills, where it would otherwise produce harmful greenhouse gases as it decomposes.

2. Soil Health: Composting returns valuable nutrients to the soil, improving its structure, fertility, and health. Healthy soil supports a thriving ecosystem of plants, insects, and microorganisms, contributing to biodiversity.

3. Water Conservation: Compost improves the soil's water-holding capacity, reducing the need for frequent watering and helping plants withstand dry conditions. This conserves water and reduces the risk of water runoff carrying pollutants into our waterways.

Benefits to Plant Health and Growth

Compost is often called "black gold" by gardeners for a good reason. It's packed with nutrients and beneficial microorganisms that enhance plant health and promote vigorous growth.

1. Nutrient-Rich: Compost slowly releases a broad spectrum of essential nutrients, providing your plants with the balanced diet they need to thrive.

2. Soil Structure: Compost helps improve soil structure by increasing its ability to retain moisture and nutrients and promoting good drainage. Whether your garden has sandy soil that drains too quickly or clay soil that holds too much water, adding compost can help.

3. Disease Resistance: Healthy soil leads to healthy plants, which can better resist pests and diseases. Compost can reduce the need for chemical pesticides and create a healthier environment for your plants.

Savings on Garden Expenses

While composting requires an initial investment of time and effort, it can lead to significant savings on garden expenses in the long run:

1. Fertilizer Savings: Compost is a free, nutrient-rich soil amendment that reduces or eliminates the need for purchased fertilizers.

2. Reduced Water Bills: As mentioned earlier, compost improves the soil's water retention capacity, meaning you need to water less frequently, saving on water bills.

3. Lower Waste Disposal Costs: By composting organic waste at home, you can reduce the volume of your household waste, potentially lowering waste disposal costs.

Overall, composting is a win-win practice. It benefits your garden, your wallet, and the planet. As a gardener, you're not just growing plants but also stewarding a tiny piece of the earth. By composting, you're doing your part to take care of it.

Mental Well-being and Composting

Interestingly, engaging in the process of composting not only benefits the environment but also can have profound positive effects on one's psychological health, fostering a range of beneficial shifts in one's mindset and well-being.

Fostering a connection with nature

Through composting, we come into direct contact with natural elements, working with organic materials and observing their miraculous transformation. This tangible interaction often rekindles our connection with nature, which can be soothing and stress-relieving. Composting can take us away from the hustle and bustle of modern life, providing us with a tranquil respite and a sense of fulfillment.

Promoting purpose and encouraging motivation

Being involved in composting is also an act of environmental responsibility. This process of converting waste into valuable resources constantly reminds us of our commitment to sustainability. It offers a sense of achievement, boosts our self-esteem, and fuels our motivation to continue adopting environmentally friendly habits. The satisfaction derived from composting and contributing positively to the environment is immeasurable.

Cultivating mindfulness and patience

composting is not instant; it requires time, observation, and patience. It allows us to witness the gradual transformation of waste into nutrient-rich compost, inspiring a slower, more thoughtful approach to life. This exposure to the gradual rhythm of nature can foster a sense of mindfulness, which can significantly benefit various aspects of our lives.

Empowering contribution to a bigger goal

Engaging in composting is a small but significant step toward minimizing pollution and mitigating climate change. It can reinforce our resilience and underline the importance and impact of individual actions. Knowing you're part of a larger, global effort can inspire hope, optimism, and empowerment.

In essence, composting is a transformative process, not just for the waste but for us as well. It enriches our psychological well-being, bolsters our commitment to environmental preservation, and intensifies our admiration for the complex cycles of nature.

Types Of Composting: An Overview Of Techniques

C omposting is versatile; it provides a variety of methods that cater to different needs, environments, and resources. It's a simple yet significant way to contribute positively to the environment by reducing waste and creating a nutrient-rich amendment for the soil.

Several techniques exist, each offering unique advantages. Some methods are suited to outdoor spaces, utilizing heaps or specialized bins to turn garden and kitchen waste into a gardener's 'black gold.'

These are excellent for households with yards, producing substantial amounts of green waste, or those wanting to reduce their carbon footprint.

Other composting techniques focus on speed, using specific conditions or elements added to hasten the decomposition process. These methods require more management but offer quicker rewards, turning waste into compost in a matter of weeks.

There are innovative composting solutions for indoor environments or those with limited space. These methods, often leveraging worms or fermentation processes, allow composting to be carried out right in the kitchen or balcony, breaking down waste, including items traditionally difficult to compost.

Furthermore, larger-scale composting techniques exist for agricultural or industrial applications. These methods deal with larger volumes of waste, often incorporating mechanical elements to handle the waste and speed up the process.

The range of composting techniques available today makes it accessible to almost everyone, irrespective of their living situation or available resources. With some knowledge and the proper method, anyone can turn their organic waste into a valuable resource, contributing to a more sustainable and circular economy.

Actually, the diversity of composting techniques demonstrates the adaptability of this process to a wide range of circumstances. In the following sections, we will delve into the details of several different composting techniques, exploring the principles underpinning each method, how they work, their unique benefits, and the practical steps involved in implementing each one.

Composting Techniques: A Quick Guide

When it comes to composting, there is no one-size-fits-all approach. Just as gardens are diverse and unique, so too are the methods of transforming waste into nutrient-rich compost. Think of composting as an art, a symbiotic dance between nature and our efforts to recycle organic waste back into the earth. Just as a dancer may perform a waltz one night and tango the next, a composter might also select different techniques based on their circumstances, needs, and materials.

Like dancers, composters also have a repertoire of moves or, in our case, techniques. This array of methods makes composting accessible to everyone, regardless of whether you have a sprawling backyard, a tiny balcony, or only a kitchen countertop. Let's take a glance at some of these methods, their benefits, and considerations. Each of these techniques will be explored in detail in subsequent chapters.

1. Traditional Composting

This is the most common method, requiring a simple compost pile or bin in your backyard. You'd add a mix of greens (nitrogen-rich materials like vegetable scraps) and browns (carbon-rich materials like leaves), and let nature do the rest. It's a straightforward technique that does not require fancy equipment.

2. Hot Composting

For the impatient gardener, hot composting might be the way to go. This technique uses thermophilic bacteria that thrive in high temperatures to decompose materials more quickly. It requires a good balance of greens and browns, frequent turning, and careful monitoring, but it can produce compost in weeks.

3. Cold Composting

This laid-back cousin of hot composting is more of a leisurely stroll than a brisk jog. In cold composting, you add materials as they become available and let the compost pile slowly decompose over a longer period. It's a low-maintenance method but requires patience.

4. Vermicomposting

This technique relies on worms (usually red wigglers) to consume organic waste and excrete castings - an exceptionally rich form of compost. Vermicomposting can be done indoors or outdoors, making it an excellent option for those with limited space.

5. Bokashi

An anaerobic process, Bokashi composting uses a specific group of microorganisms to ferment organic waste in a sealed container. It's a speedy method that can handle types of waste typically avoided in traditional composting, such as dairy and cooked food.

6. Trench Composting

Here, you dig a trench in your garden, fill it with compostable materials, and then cover it with soil. The compost decomposes directly in the ground, enriching the soil where your plants will grow. It's a stealthy and effective way of composting, handy if you don't want a visible compost pile.

7. Sheet Composting

Also known as "lasagna composting," this method involves layering greens and browns directly onto a garden bed and leaving them to decompose over time. It's a wonderful technique for improving soil directly where you plan to plant.

As we delve deeper into each of these methods in the pages to come, you'll gain a thorough understanding of their workings and nuances, and you'll be well-equipped to choose the method (or methods) that suit your unique situation and composting goals. The beauty of composting lies in its flexibility and adaptability to diverse circumstances. It's a practice where the journey and the destination are equally enriching.

The need for diverse composting methods

Organic waste, which makes up a substantial portion of our waste stream, is generated in all types of settings, from rural to urban, from homes to businesses, and from small gardens to large farms. The necessity for multiple composting techniques results from people and communities having different needs, resources, and objectives. Different composting methods can cater to these different contexts and conditions, making composting an accessible and beneficial practice for everyone.

1. Spatial Considerations: The amount of available space is a significant factor that dictates the composting method one can employ. Traditional composting, for example, usually requires a backyard or outdoor area to accommodate a compost heap or bin. This method might be suitable for suburban or rural areas but might not be feasible for someone living in a high-rise apartment in a big city. Urban dwellers can choose vermicomposting or bokashi composting, which can be done in small containers indoors.

2. Type and Volume of Waste: The kind and quantity of organic waste generated also influence the choice of composting method. Traditional composting or trench composting can handle large amounts of yard waste like leaves, grass clippings, and branches, making these methods suitable for individuals with large yards or gardens. On the other hand, vermicomposting is an excellent choice for kitchen scraps but not for yard waste. Bokashi composting can handle a broader range of waste, including meat and dairy products, which are typically not recommended for other composting methods due to the risk of attracting pests.

3. Time and Maintenance: Different composting methods require varying degrees of time and maintenance. Traditional composting, for instance, requires regular turning of the compost pile and careful balancing of 'green' and 'brown' materials. Vermicomposting also requires some care, including feeding the worms and maintaining the right temperature and moisture levels. Bokashi composting involves a two-step process of fermentation and then composting. Trench composting, on the other hand, is relatively low maintenance. Once the organic waste is buried, nature does the rest. The choice of method can therefore depend on how much time and effort an individual is willing or able to dedicate to composting.

4. Climate: The local climate can also influence the choice of composting method. Traditional composting, for example, can be slower in colder climates. In contrast, vermicomposting and bokashi composting can be done indoors, making them not as dependent on outside weather conditions.

5. End Use of Compost: The intended use for the finished compost can also influence the choice of composting method. For example, vermicomposting produces worm castings, which are highly nutrient-rich and beneficial for growing plants in containers. On the other hand, Bokashi composting results in a type of compost that is particularly well-suited for improving the soil in gardens or larger agricultural settings.

Hot and Cold Composting

When entering the world of composting, you'll soon discover there's more than one way to turn those kitchen scraps and garden waste into black gold for your plants. Two of the most popular methods are hot and cold composting, each with its own unique advantages and approach. Let's dive in and explore the differences between these two techniques.

Hot Composting

Imagine, if you will, a bustling city that never sleeps; a metropolis where the energy is palpable and constant. That's hot composting for you. It's the rapid transit system of the composting world - a little high maintenance, perhaps, but it delivers results at top speed.

The Basics of Hot Composting

Hot composting involves piling organic waste into a heap or bin and allowing it to heat up, typically between 130-160°F (54-71°C). This is no lazy Sunday afternoon barbecue, though - you aim to create conditions where thermophilic (heat-loving) bacteria can thrive and rapidly break down the waste.

Hot composting requires a careful balance of 'green' materials (rich in nitrogen, such as vegetable scraps and grass clippings) and 'brown' materials (rich in carbon, such as dried leaves and newspaper). A ratio of about 1:2 (greens to browns) is generally recommended.

Steps to Create a Hot Compost Pile

1. Start the Pile: You'll need a fair amount of material to kick things off - ideally at least 3x3x3 feet. Layer your greens and browns, chop or shred larger pieces to help them break down faster.

2. Turn the Pile: Turn the compost pile every few days with a pitchfork or compost aerator. This introduces oxygen, essential for composting, and ensures the heap heats evenly.

3. Monitor the Temperature: Check the compost temperature regularly. When it drops below 130°F (54°C), it's time to turn the pile.

4. Finish the Process: After about a month, your compost should be ready. It'll look like rich, dark soil and have a pleasant, earthy smell.

Pros and Cons of Hot Composting

The main advantage of hot composting is speed. This could be your method if you're keen to get composting and need results fast. Hot composting also has the added benefit of killing most weed seeds and pathogens, due to the high temperatures involved.

However, hot composting can be labor-intensive. It requires regular turning and monitoring. You'll also need a large volume of materials to start.

Cold Composting

On the other end of the spectrum, we have cold composting. It's the serene countryside to hot composting's bustling city - a slower, more relaxed method that gently hums along in the background of your garden.

The Basics of Cold Composting

Cold composting, also known as passive composting, is a more leisurely approach. Add organic materials to your compost pile or bin as they become available and let nature take its course. This method primarily relies on mesophilic organisms, which work best at lower temperatures.

Like hot composting, cold composting benefits from a balance of greens and browns, although the process is more forgiving if the ratio isn't perfect.

Steps to Create a Cold Compost Pile

1. Start the Pile: Start your compost pile in a corner of your yard, a compost bin, or even a large trash can with some holes drilled in it for ventilation. Start adding your greens and browns as you accumulate them.

2. Turn the Pile (Optional): Turning the pile is optional with cold composting. Doing so can speed up the process, but it isn't necessary.

3. Wait for the Magic: Patience is key here. Depending on your climate and the materials you're composting, it can take anywhere from six months to two years to fully compost.

4. Finish the Process: When the material at the bottom of your pile looks like dark, crumbly soil and smells earthy, it's ready to use.

<u>Pros and Cons of Cold Composting</u>

The biggest advantage of cold composting is its simplicity. It's a set-it-and-forget-it process that requires little maintenance. It's also suitable for smaller quantities of waste and doesn't demand the immediate volume that hot composting does.

However, cold composting takes longer to produce finished compost. The lower temperatures also mean it's less likely to kill weed seeds and disease-causing organisms.

In conclusion, both hot and cold composting offer viable ways to recycle organic waste into a valuable resource for your garden. Whether you prefer the rapid results of hot composting or the laid-back simplicity of cold composting, the important thing is that you're helping to reduce waste and create healthier soil. It's truly a win-win for you and the environment.

Aerobic vs. Anaerobic Composting

Delving into composting further, we find two primary approaches: aerobic and anaerobic composting.

Aerobic Composting

Aerobic composting is probably what comes to mind when most people think of composting. This method gets its name from the aerobic bacteria - those that require oxygen to survive - doing most of the decomposition work.

Here's how the process generally works: You start by creating a mix of 'green' nitrogen-rich materials (like vegetable scraps, coffee grounds, or fresh grass clippings) and 'brown' carbon-rich materials (like dried leaves, straw, or shredded paper). You then turn or stir this pile every week or two. Turning aims to aerate the pile, providing oxygen to the bacteria and enabling them to work effectively.

The beauty of aerobic composting is that it can break down waste relatively quickly. You can expect to have usable compost within a few months. It also generates heat, killing pathogens and weed seeds, making the resulting compost safer for your garden. When done correctly, the process is generally odor-free, as the aerobic bacteria produce carbon dioxide, not methane (which smells).

Anaerobic Composting

On the other hand, Anaerobic composting is a decomposition process that occurs without oxygen. It's conducted by anaerobic bacteria, which, unlike their aerobic counterparts, don't need oxygen to survive. You might encounter this type of composting if you've ever come across a sealed composting bin or a compost pile that hasn't been turned in a while.

The advantage of anaerobic composting is that it's less labor-intensive since it doesn't require turning. This might make it attractive for those who want a more hands-off approach to composting.

However, anaerobic composting has its downsides. The process is typically slower than aerobic composting, taking six months to a year to produce finished compost. It also tends to produce odors because the anaerobic bacteria release gases like methane and hydrogen sulfide (the rotten egg smell) during decomposition.

Similarities and Differences

While both aerobic and anaerobic composting serve the same purpose (transforming organic waste into useful compost), their methodologies differ. They both break down organic material, but the processes, timelines, and byproducts vary significantly.

Aerobic composting requires more work (turning the pile), but it's faster, usually more efficient, and less likely to produce unpleasant odors. Anaerobic composting, while less labor-intensive, takes longer, is often less efficient, and can produce more odors.

In summary, deciding between aerobic and anaerobic composting comes down to your individual needs, preferences, and how much effort you're willing to put into your composting process. Both methods can effectively recycle organic waste into valuable compost, reducing waste and creating a healthier garden.

The Science Behind Composting: A Look At The Microscopic World

P icture this: an active ecosystem full of vitality, where each member actively contributes to the health of the whole. Each participant, from the smallest to the most influential, aids in converting raw substances into precious assets. This is not a representation of human civilization but a depiction of the activity within the minuscule universe of a compost pile.

Introduction to Compost Microbiology

Composting, without a doubt, is an example of nature's resourcefulness and efficiency. Although to our eyes, it may seem like we're merely observing waste slowly become a rich, earthy substance, the true magic of composting happens at a microscopic level. This hidden world is the domain of compost microbiology, a fascinating field of study that unravels the roles of billions of organisms that are the true heroes of the composting process.

Understanding the microscopic aspect of composting allows us to appreciate and manage the process more effectively. After all, we're dealing with living organisms with specific needs. They require a certain amount of heat, moisture, and air and a balanced diet of carbon and nitrogen-rich materials. When their needs are met, they work rapidly to decompose organic matter, generating heat, carbon dioxide, and water as by-products.

If the conditions aren't desirable, decomposition slows down or stops altogether. Or worse, the wrong kind of microorganisms can take over, leading to foul smells and poor-quality compost. By understanding the needs and activities of compost microorganisms, we can create the ideal conditions for them to do their work. In a sense, we become the mayors of our own microscopic cities, responsible for ensuring that the infrastructure and resources are in place for the inhabitants to thrive.

So, let's take a closer look at this microscopic world, learning about its workings, inhabitants, and importance. By doing so, we'll become better composters and gain a deeper appreciation for the complex and interconnected processes that sustain life on our planet.

Bacteria: The Composting Workhorse

While a compost pile hosts a diverse cast of microscopic organisms, including fungi, protozoa, and even small animals like nematodes and mites, it's the bacteria that take center stage. They are the workhorses of composting, the tireless toilers that break down organic matter into its constituent parts, paving the way for other decomposing organisms.

Role of Bacteria in Composting

Bacteria act as nature's little recyclers. They are the first and most numerous settlers within your compost pile, eagerly starting the decomposition process.

If you're a newbie to the field, you might wonder, "What exactly does it mean for bacteria to decompose organic matter?" Well, bacteria produce specialized proteins known as enzymes, which can be considered tiny molecular machines. These enzymes attach to complex organic molecules, such as cellulose in a dead leaf or proteins in kitchen scraps, and break them into simpler compounds. This process, known as enzymatic degradation, is similar to how our bodies break down food.

As bacteria break down these complex molecules, they absorb the resulting simpler compounds, which serve as their fuel. They use this fuel to grow, reproduce, and continue their work within the compost pile.

Bacteria also produce some by-products. They release heat, a characteristic trait of a healthy compost pile that aids decomposition. The heat they generate is a result of their metabolism, a term referring to the multitude of chemical reactions occurring within their cells to maintain life.

They also generate water and carbon dioxide, both of which contribute to the composting process. The water they produce helps keep the compost pile's moisture level, which is a vital factor for composting. Meanwhile, the carbon dioxide they release is a harmless gas that goes back into the atmosphere, contributing to the carbon cycle.

Different Types of Composting Bacteria

Bacteria in the compost pile can be generally classified into three groups based on the temperatures at which they thrive: psychrophilic, mesophilic, and thermophilic bacteria.

1. Psychrophilic Bacteria: These are the first responders of the compost pile, jumping into action as soon as there's enough food available. Psychrophilic bacteria work best at cooler temperatures, between 0°C and 20°C (32°F and 68°F), and start the process of breaking down the organic matter in the compost pile.

2. Mesophilic Bacteria: As the compost pile starts to heat up, thanks to the activities of the psychrophilic bacteria, the mesophilic bacteria take over. They thrive at temperatures between 20°C and 45°C (68°F and 113°F) and are responsible for much of the decomposition that occurs in a compost pile. Mesophilic bacteria break down proteins, sugars, and starches in the organic waste, producing heat as a by-product and further causing the compost pile's temperature to rise.

3. Thermophilic Bacteria: The thermophilic bacteria step in once the compost pile's temperature gets above 45°C (113°F). These high-temperature lovers can work at temperatures up to 70°C (158°F) and break down more resistant materials like fats, cellulose, and even some forms of lignin. The activities of thermophilic bacteria turn a compost pile into a hot pile, killing off weed seeds and disease-causing organisms. However, if the pile gets too hot, it can also kill off the beneficial microorganisms, so careful management is a must.

Understanding these different types of bacteria and their roles in composting allows us to better manage our compost piles. By ensuring a good balance of green and brown materials, maintaining the proper moisture levels, and turning the pile to provide adequate oxygen, we can create the ideal conditions for these beneficial bacteria to operate best, speeding up the composting process and producing high-quality compost for our gardens.

Fungi and Mold in the Compost Pile

The composting process involves a variety of microscopic creatures, and among them, fungi and mold play significant roles. While they might not be as immediately active as bacteria, their impact on the composting process is substantial.

Fungi and mold participate in composting, particularly in its later stages. When the early-stage bacteria have consumed the easy-to-decompose materials and the heat in the compost pile has subsided, fungi and mold start their decomposition.

Their main targets are cellulose and lignin, which provide a rigid structure to plant cells. Because of their toughness, these materials resist decay and require specific decomposers to break them down.

This is where fungi and mold make their mark. They produce specialized enzymes that break down tough materials such as cellulose and lignin into simpler compounds. Their decomposition abilities help to ensure that even the most resilient plant materials are turned into nutrient-rich compost.

When you observe white, blue, or green fuzzy patches on your compost pile, it's usually fungi or mold at work. Their appearance is not something to worry about but rather a positive sign. It indicates that your compost pile is functioning well and the decomposition process is progressing effectively.

The Balance of Organisms

In a well-functioning compost pile, there's a balance between the different types of microorganisms. Bacteria, fungi, and mold all work together, each taking on different roles in the decomposition process.

Bacteria are the first to start the process, breaking down the easily decomposable organic material. Fungi and mold follow, dealing with the more complex materials. This division of labor assists in efficiently breaking all organic material in the compost pile.

Keeping this balance of organisms is one of the keys to successful composting. You can do this by providing a good mix of green and brown materials, turning the compost pile regularly to maintain oxygen levels, and keeping the compost pile moist but not too wet. By doing these things, you'll create a welcoming environment for all the microorganisms in your compost pile and ensure a successful composting process.

Larger Organisms: Worms, Beetles, and More

While the microscopic world is the primary driver of composting, it's not the whole story. A host of larger organisms also make their homes in compost piles, contributing to the decomposition process in important ways. These larger inhabitants of your compost pile, such as worms, beetles, and other insects, often get less attention, but their roles are crucial in maintaining a healthy compost ecosystem.

The Roles These Creatures Play in the Composting Process

- Worms: Earthworms are the superstars of composting. In a process known as vermicomposting, worms eat organic material, breaking it down into smaller components as they chew and digest it. As they tunnel through the compost, they also help to mix the materials and incorporate oxygen into the pile, which aids the aerobic decomposition process. The worm castings (worm poop) left behind are rich in nutrients and beneficial microbes, making them a valuable addition to the compost.

- Beetles and Other Insects: Beetles, especially rove beetles and ground beetles, along with other insects like sow bugs and springtails, facilitate the composting process. They help break down larger organic material into smaller pieces that bacteria and fungi can more easily decompose. These critters also serve as a food source for other organisms, contributing to the overall biodiversity and health of the compost pile.

- Centipedes and Millipedes: Centipedes are carnivores and help control the population of other insects in the compost pile. Millipedes, on the other hand, are decomposers and contribute to breaking down organic material.

- Arachnids: Spiders and mites, while not everyone's favorite, play important parts in the compost pile. They keep the population of other insects in check, which assists in maintaining the balance of organisms. Some mites also help decompose organic material.

- Birds: Birds don't live in the compost pile but may be among frequent visitors, picking off insects and other small creatures. This can aid in the control of insect populations.

These larger organisms are an essential part of the compost ecosystem. They help break down and mix the compost, contribute to its nutrient content, and help maintain the balance of organisms in the compost pile. So next time you turn your compost pile and see a worm or beetle, be gentle because they're doing their work.

Maintaining a Healthy Compost Ecosystem

As you might have realized by now, composting is a complex ecological process that relies on the balance and diversity of a multitude of micro and macro-organisms. That's why maintaining a healthy compost ecosystem is vital to ensure the efficient breakdown of organic materials into nutrient-rich compost.

Factors that can Influence the Microbial Balance

- Temperature: Different organisms thrive at different temperatures. For instance, certain bacteria prefer cooler temperatures, while others are more active in heat. If the compost pile gets too hot or too cold, it can disturb the balance of organisms.

- Moisture: Water is essential for the life processes of composting organisms, but too much or too little can be problematic. If the compost pile is too wet, it can become anaerobic (lacking oxygen), leading to unpleasant smells and slow decomposition. If it's too dry, the organisms can become dormant.

- Aeration: Composting organisms need oxygen to survive. Without proper aeration, the compost pile can become anaerobic, slowing down the composting process and leading to foul odors.

- pH Level: The acidity or alkalinity of the compost pile can affect the types of organisms that can thrive. Most composting organisms prefer a near-neutral pH.

- Carbon-Nitrogen Ratio: Composting organisms need a balanced diet of carbon for energy and nitrogen for growth. An imbalance in this ratio can slow the composting process and affect the organisms' balance.

How to Nurture the Microscopic Life in Your Compost Pile

- Balance Green and Brown Materials: Green materials provide nitrogen, while brown materials provide carbon. A good ratio to aim for is about 2:1 browns to greens by volume.

- Maintain Moisture Levels: Your compost pile should be as damp as a wrung-out sponge. If it's too dry, add water or green materials. If it's too wet, add brown materials or turn the pile to improve aeration.

- Turn the Pile Regularly: Turning the pile helps incorporate oxygen, which is vital for the aerobic bacteria that drive the composting process. It also helps distribute moisture and heat evenly throughout the pile.

- Add a Variety of Materials: A diverse diet will support a diverse microbial community. Different materials will attract different types of organisms, accelerating the composting process and improving the quality of the finished compost.

- Avoid Toxic Substances: Certain materials, like treated wood, certain kinds of manure, or any substance containing harmful chemicals, can kill beneficial composting organisms and should be avoided.

By understanding the needs of the composting organisms and providing a favorable environment, you can nurture the microscopic life in your compost pile and create a healthy, thriving compost ecosystem.

BOOK II

COMPOST MADE EASY

A BEGINNER'S GUIDE TO CRAFTING NUTRIENT-RICH SOIL

Diving into the world of composting is like embarking on a mini adventure right in your backyard. It's a journey of transformation that reduces waste, enriches your garden, and connects you more deeply with nature's cycles.

Now, if you're ready to immerse yourself in this rewarding practice, let's start from the very beginning.

Setting Up Your Composting System

W elcome to the insightful guide to green living that emphasizes the significance and process of composting. This five-step manual provides a comprehensive overview of setting up your compost area, from the initial stage of choosing the right location, selecting an appropriate compost bin, adding the right materials, maintaining the compost pile, and finally waiting for the transformation. It underscores the need for balance, patience, and regular maintenance in creating nutrient-rich compost, a sustainable alternative to chemical fertilizers that improves soil health, supports plant growth, and conserves water.

Mastering Compost: A Step-by-Step Guide

Choose the Right Location

When choosing a spot for your compost, finding a balance between convenience and suitability is key. The location should be easily accessible, as you'll add materials regularly and maintain the pile. Good drainage prevents the compost pile from becoming overly saturated and smelly. A spot near a water source can also be beneficial when the pile needs additional moisture. Lastly, a partially shaded place is ideal as it helps keep the compost from drying out during hot weather while preventing excess moisture buildup during rainy periods.

Select a Compost Bin or Create a Compost Heap

Various compost bins are available, and each offers unique benefits. The right choice depends on your space constraints, the volume of waste, and personal preference. Tumblers, for instance, are easy to turn and can help speed up the composting process. Stationary bins are generally larger and can be a great choice if you have a high volume of waste. Alternatively, you can also create a compost heap directly on the ground, which is a cost-effective and traditional method. Just make sure to maintain it well to avoid attracting pests.

Start Adding Your Compost Materials

The key to effective composting lies in balancing green (nitrogen-rich) and brown (carbon-rich) materials. Green materials, such as fruit and vegetable scraps, coffee grounds, and fresh grass clippings, provide the necessary nitrogen for the composting organisms, while brown materials, such as dry leaves, straw, and shredded newspaper, provide carbon, which gives the microbes energy to process the nitrogen. Starting your pile with a layer of browns promotes aeration and drainage, while a layer of greens on top introduces nitrogen. Continue alternating these layers for the best results.

Maintain Your Compost Pile

Compost piles require regular maintenance to speed up decomposition. This can be done using a pitchfork or a specialized compost turner. Turning the pile every few weeks ensures that all materials get exposed to the center of the pile, where the heat and activity are most significant. Monitoring moisture levels is also critical. If the compost appears too dry, adding some water is advised since the composting organisms depend on moisture for survival. Conversely, if it's too wet, adding more brown material can help absorb excess moisture and restore balance in the pile.

Wait and Watch

Patience is a must when it comes to composting. Using compost in your garden reduces the need for chemical fertilizers, improves soil structure, promotes healthy plant growth, and conserves water by helping the soil retain moisture. Over several weeks to a few months, depending on the materials used and the weather conditions, your compost pile will transform into a rich, dark material that closely resembles fertile garden soil. This is your finished compost, ready to enrich your garden or pots.

Composting Materials: What You Can and Can't Compost

Composting is a versatile process that can accommodate various organic materials. However, knowing what can and can't be composted is crucial to keeping a healthy compost pile and ensuring the end product is safe for your garden. Here, we'll delve into the specifics.

What You Can Compost

- Green Materials: Also known as nitrogen-rich materials, these are fundamental to the composting process. They supply the necessary nutrients for composting microbes, serving as their protein source. Typical green materials include fruit and vegetable scraps, a rich nitrogen and moisture source. Coffee grounds and tea bags are other everyday kitchen waste that falls into this category. Fresh grass clippings and green plant prunings from your garden also fit into the 'greens' category. It's worth noting that these materials decompose quickly, raising the compost pile's temperature and speeding up the composting process.

- Brown Materials: Often referred to as carbon-rich materials, these elements are equally vital for successful composting. They provide the energy composting microbes need to break down the green materials. In a sense, these brown materials are like carbohydrates in the microbes' diet. Examples of brown materials include dried leaves, usually abundant in the fall and an excellent carbon source. Straw can also serve as a brown material, adding structure to your compost pile. Shredded newspaper, cardboard, and sawdust are other common examples of brown materials. However, when using newspaper and cardboard, make sure they are not coated with any plastic or harmful chemicals. Balancing these brown materials with green ones is essential to maintain a healthy compost pile.

- Other Compostable Materials: Some items do not neatly fit into the green or brown categories but can be valuable additions to your compost pile. For instance, eggshells can be composted, and while they decompose slowly, they add calcium to the compost, an essential nutrient for plant growth. Hair and fur, both pet and human, can also be composted; these materials are rich in nitrogen and decompose reasonably quickly. Moreover, your compost pile can include 100% cotton or wool rags. They break down over time, but it's necessary to verify that they don't contain any synthetic materials or harmful chemicals. Always cut or tear these rags into smaller pieces to help speed up the decomposition process. This variety of materials ensures that your compost pile is rich in diverse nutrients, significantly benefiting the plants that will ultimately receive this compost.

What You Can't Compost

While many materials can be composted, as I mentioned previously, there are some things you should avoid adding to your compost pile:

- Meat and Dairy Products: These can attract pests and create unpleasant odors as they decompose.

- Diseased Plants or Weeds with Seeds: These might not get hot enough to kill the disease or seeds, and you could end up spreading the problem when you use your compost.

- Pet Waste: Dog or cat feces can contain harmful pathogens that may not be killed during composting.

- Chemically Treated Wood Products: These can leach harmful chemicals into your compost.

- Anything Inorganic: This includes plastics, metals, and glass. They do not decompose and can contaminate your compost.

It's worth noting that composting requirements can vary depending on your specific composting method. For instance, some methods like Bokashi composting can handle meat and dairy products. As always, it's essential to research and understand the needs and limitations of your chosen composting system.

Understanding Green and Brown Materials

The interplay between green and brown materials keeps the composting process efficient and productive. An imbalance in this equation can lead to less-than-desirable outcomes. For instance, too many greens can create an overly wet compost pile that gives off a foul smell, a clear sign that the materials are decomposing anaerobically without enough oxygen. On the other hand, a compost pile with excessive browns can slow down the decomposition process, as there isn't enough nitrogen to fuel the microbial activity needed to break down the materials.

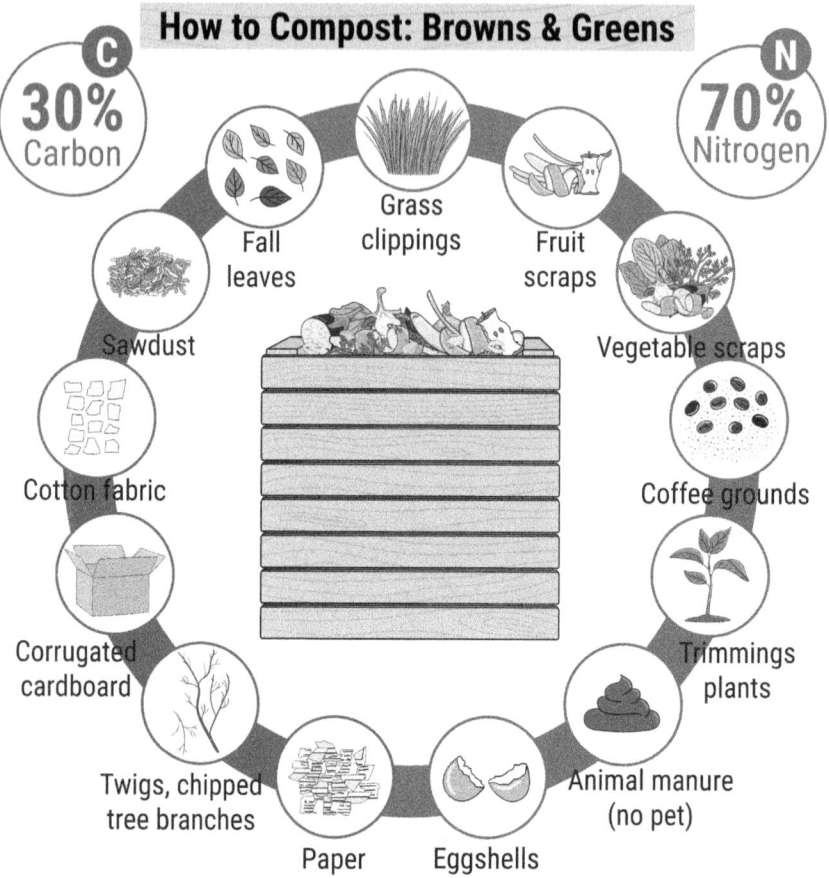

How to Compost: Browns & Greens

C 30% Carbon

N 70% Nitrogen

Fall leaves · Grass clippings · Fruit scraps · Vegetable scraps · Sawdust · Coffee grounds · Cotton fabric · Corrugated cardboard · Twigs, chipped tree branches · Paper · Eggshells · Animal manure (no pet) · Trimmings plants

- Green Materials: Characterized by their nitrogen-rich composition, green materials are the protein providers for the bustling community of microbes breaking down the compost pile. Typically moist in nature, these include a variety of items commonly found in your kitchen or garden, such as fruit and vegetable scraps, coffee grounds, tea bags, fresh grass clippings, and young, green plant material. These items infuse your compost with nitrogen, a crucial element that drives microbial activity and accelerates decomposition.

- Brown Materials: On the other side of the scale are brown materials. Browns are usually dry, including dry leaves, straw, cardboard, shredded newspaper, and even small branches. These carbon-rich substances provide the necessary energy for the composting microbes and play a significant role in balancing the moisture content in your compost pile. The carbon from these materials not only fuels the microbes but also aids in forming the structure of the compost pile, promoting aeration and preventing it from becoming compacted and waterlogged.

Here's a list of common browns and greens you can use in your composting endeavors:

Browns (Carbon-rich materials)

- Fallen leaves

- Straw

- Newspaper (shredded or torn into small pieces)

- Cardboard (shredded or torn into small pieces)

- Wood chips or sawdust

- Pine needles

- Dry grass clippings

- Cornstalks

- Twigs and small branches (broken into smaller pieces)

- Eggshells (crushed)

- Peat moss

Greens (Nitrogen-rich materials)

Vegetable scraps

Fruit scraps

Coffee grounds

Tea leaves or tea bags (remove any staples or plastic)

Fresh grass clippings

Green plant trimmings

Weeds (avoid those with seeds or invasive roots)

Manure (from herbivores like cows, horses, or chickens)

Hair and fur (from pets or hairbrushes)

Feathers

Seaweed or algae (rinsed to remove salt)

Achieving the Right Balance

A general rule of thumb in composting circles is to aim for a ratio of 2:1 browns to greens by volume. This ratio serves as a guideline rather than a rigid requirement, and the ideal balance can shift depending on the specific materials you're compost-ing, local weather conditions, and other factors. However, composting is an organic process influenced by numerous variables and isn't bound by strict mathematical rules. Don't hesitate to experiment and discover what works best for your specific situation and composting goals.

But why is this balance so important? Too many greens and your compost pile may turn into a smelly mess. Too many browns and the composting process slows to a snail's pace. The goal here is to target a mix in your compost pile that's about one-third greens and two-thirds browns. This translates to adding one portion of green materials for every two portions of browns.

Imagine your green materials are primarily composed of fruit and vegetable peels and scraps, while your brown materials are dry leaves and small branches. What you'll do is create your compost heap by layering these materials, alternating between thin layers of browns and greens. Proceed until you've incorporated all your kitchen waste and two heaps of your dry garden waste into the pile.

Tips and Tricks for Success

Here are some tips and tricks to help you create rich, healthy compost more efficiently.

Striking the Right Balance

Composting is a bit like cooking—you need the right ingredients in the right proportions. The "greens" are nitrogen-rich materials like vegetable peels, coffee grounds, and fresh grass clippings. They're the life of the party, providing the protein that the composting microbes need to grow.

The "browns" are carbon-rich materials like dried leaves, straw, or shredded paper. They're the chaperones at the compost party, providing the energy the microbes need to do their work.

Remember, balance is vital in the compost world! A good compost pile needs greens and browns; generally, you want about twice as many browns as greens. So, you'd add two buckets of dried leaves or straw for every bucket of vegetable peels and coffee grounds.

The Power of Small Pieces

Here's a little composting secret: size matters. The smaller the pieces in your compost pile, the faster they decompose. Why? Because smaller pieces have more surface area, which means more room for the composting microbes to do their thing.

So, if you want to speed up the composting process, try chopping or shredding your materials before you add them to the pile. This can be as simple as tearing up cardboard boxes or chopping kitchen scraps into smaller pieces. It might take a little extra time, but your compost pile will thank you!

Why Turning Matters

Composting is not a set-it-and-forget-it type of thing. It needs a bit of tender loving care now and then, and one of the best ways to show your compost some love is by turning it regularly. Turning your compost pile helps to aerate it, introducing much-needed oxygen that helps the composting microbes thrive.

Think of it like stirring a pot of soup. It helps distribute the heat evenly and ensures all ingredients are cooked properly. The same goes for your compost pile. By turning it every few weeks, you're helping to speed up the decomposition process and create a more uniform compost.

Not Too Dry, Not Too Wet

Here's another important tip: your compost pile should be moist but not soggy. The composting microbes need water to survive, but too much of it can drown them and cause your compost pile to become smelly and anaerobic.

So, what's the right amount of water? Well, your compost pile should feel like a wrung-out sponge. It should be damp but not dripping wet. If it's too dry, add some water or more green materials. If it's too wet, add more browns to help absorb the excess moisture.

The Composting No-Nos

While composting is a fantastic way to recycle many kinds of organic waste, there are some things that you should keep out of your compost pile. Meat, dairy products, and pet waste can attract pests, create unpleasant odors, and introduce harmful pathogens into your compost. Similarly, diseased plants and chemically treated wood products can introduce toxins that could harm your plants and soil.

So, when in doubt, leave it out! It's better to be safe than sorry, especially when it comes to creating a healthy compost for your garden.

The Waiting Game

Composting is a natural process; like all natural processes, it takes time. Depending on the materials you're composting and the conditions in your compost pile, it could take a few weeks to several months for your compost to be ready.

So be patient, my fellow composters! Trust in the process and the hard work of the billions of tiny microbes turning your waste into garden gold.

From Pile to Garden

When your compost has transformed into a rich, dark, crumbly material that smells like fresh earth, it's time to celebrate—because you've got finished compost! This garden gold is ready to use in your garden beds, to mix into potting soil, or to serve as a natural mulch.

Essential Tools for Composting: Containers and Equipment

Composting can be as simple or as complex as you want. Let's take a look at some essential containers and tools that can make your composting experience smoother, more efficient, and, dare we say, even more fun.

Choosing the Right Bin or Tumbler

The heart of your composting operation will be your compost bin or tumbler. This is where the magic happens: your kitchen scraps and garden waste transform into nutrient-rich compost for your garden. So, choosing the right container is a big deal.

Compost bins come in all shapes and sizes, from repurposed trash cans to specially designed composting units. Some people prefer the simplicity of a stationary bin, which basically just sits there and lets nature do its thing.

Others might opt for a compost tumbler, like a compost bin on steroids. With a compost tumbler, you can easily turn your compost just by spinning the tumbler, which can help speed up the composting process. Plus, they're often rodent-proof, which is a big plus if you live in an area with curious critters.

Choosing the right container depends on your space, budget, and composting needs. There's no one-size-fits-all solution, so take some time to consider what would work best for you.

Why You Need a Compost Pail

Here's a little secret: not all composting happens outside. A lot of it starts right in your kitchen! Keeping a small compost pail in your kitchen makes collecting fruit and vegetable scraps, coffee grounds, eggshells, and other compostable materials easy.

Look for a compost pail with a tight-fitting lid to keep any smells contained and a handle for easy carrying. Some even come with a carbon filter to help control odors. You'd be surprised how quickly those scraps can add up, and every bit helps in creating rich, fertile compost.

The Pitchfork and Compost Turner

Now, let's talk about turning. You've probably heard that regularly turning your compost pile is good. It helps introduce oxygen into the pile, mixes the materials, and speeds up composting. But how do you actually do it? Enter the pitchfork and compost turner.

A garden pitchfork is a versatile tool that can be used for turning your compost pile. It's good for getting deep into the pile and giving it a good mix. Plus, it's a great workout!

If you want to take it up a notch, you might consider a compost-turner. These specially designed tools have a unique corkscrew design, making turning your compost pile easier and more efficient. Simply push the turner into your pile and twist - it's like giving your compost pile a good stir!

A Garden Hose with a Spray Nozzle

Water is a crucial part of the composting process. Your compost pile needs to be kept moist but not too wet. Think "damp sponge" rather than "soaked towel." A garden hose with a spray nozzle makes it easy to give your compost pile a quick spritz if it's looking a little dry. Plus, it's a great way to cool off on a hot day!

A Wheelbarrow

Once your compost is ready to use, you'll need a way to get it from your compost pile to your garden beds. Enter the humble wheelbarrow. This simple tool can save you a lot of heavy lifting and makes transporting your finished compost a breeze. Plus, it's also handy for all sorts of other garden tasks. Trust me, and your back will thank you!

Gloves and Boots

When composting, getting your hands (and feet) a little dirty is part of the fun. But sometimes, you might appreciate a bit of protection. That's where gloves and boots come in.

Gloves are not strictly necessary for composting, but they can make the process more comfortable, especially if you're handling a large compost pile. They protect your hands from potential irritants and keep them clean(ish) during the process. Plus, gloves can give you a better grip and prevent blisters if you're using a pitchfork or compost turner.

Boots, on the other hand (or should we say foot?), are great for those days when you're trudging out to your compost pile in the rain or snow or turning a particularly messy pile. Look for sturdy, waterproof boots that can withstand the elements. Your feet will stay dry and comfortable, and you won't track compost back into the house.

Debunking Common Misconceptions About Composting

Composting is an excellent way to reduce your carbon footprint, enhance your garden's soil health, and minimize household waste. Many beginners shy away from composting despite its numerous benefits due to widespread misconceptions. Here,

I aim to debunk some of these myths and offer reassurance that composting can be rewarding.

1. Composting is Smelly

One of the most pervasive myths about composting is that it generates unpleasant odors. While it's true that an improperly maintained compost pile can produce bad smells, a well-managed compost pile should not.

Here's the deal: composting is a process guided by nature. The decomposition process is odor-free when you have the right balance of green materials (like vegetable peels, coffee grounds, or grass clippings) and brown materials (like dried leaves, straw, or paper).

The unpleasant smell usually arises when the compost pile lacks enough oxygen, often due to excess moisture or a lack of brown materials. If the compost pile becomes anaerobic (lacks oxygen), odor-causing bacteria can take over. But, by maintaining a balanced compost pile and turning it regularly to allow aeration, you can prevent this issue.

2. Composting Attracts Pests

The idea that composting invites pests, like rodents and bugs, is another misconception. Although compost piles can be a food source for pests, a well-maintained compost bin shouldn't attract more pests than any other part of your yard.

Most pests won't be interested if you're diligent about what you compost. For example, avoid composting meats, dairy, or cooked food scraps, as these items attract pests. Stick to plant-based scraps, coffee grounds, eggshells, and yard waste.

Using a compost bin with a lid or turning your compost pile regularly also helps to discourage pests, as does burying food waste under a layer of brown materials.

3. Composting is Complicated

Many people believe composting is a complex scientific process requiring precise measurement and timing. While composting does involve some science, you don't need to be a scientist to do it successfully.

Think of composting as a recipe with two main ingredients: greens and browns. Greens provide nitrogen and are materials like vegetable scraps, coffee grounds, or grass clippings. Browns provide carbon, including materials like dried leaves, straw, or shredded newspaper.

The general rule is to aim for a ratio of about 2:1 browns to greens by volume. However, don't be discouraged if you can't maintain this ratio perfectly. Composting is flexible and forgiving. If you notice that your pile is becoming smelly (too many greens) or isn't decomposing (too many browns), you can simply adjust the ratio.

4. Composting is Time-Consuming

Another misconception is that composting requires a lot of time. In reality, the amount of time you'll spend on composting is minimal. After setting up your compost pile or bin, you only need a few minutes each day or even every few days to add materials and give the pile a turn to promote aeration.

Keep in mind that composting is a natural process. Whether you intervene or not, organic materials will decompose over time. Your role in composting is simply to provide the right conditions (balance of materials and aeration) to speed up the process.

5. Composting Requires a Large Space

You might think composting requires a large backyard, but this is untrue. Size doesn't have to be a barrier to composting. Composting can be done in a small bin on a balcony, in a worm composting system in your kitchen, or even in a shared community composting facility.

Indoor composting systems, like worm bins or Bokashi bins, are a great solution for those living in apartments or homes with small yards. When managed correctly, these methods are efficient, compact, and don't produce unpleasant odors.

A traditional compost bin or tumbler can be an excellent choice for those with slightly more space, like a balcony or small yard. These systems are enclosed, which helps to prevent any potential issues with pests or odors, and they come in a range of sizes to suit different space constraints.

Community composting is another fantastic option for those lacking space. Many cities have community gardens or programs that accept kitchen scraps for their composting projects. This can also be a great way to meet like-minded community members and learn more about composting.

Composting is an environmentally-friendly, rewarding practice that can be incorporated into various lifestyles and living situations. The myths surrounding composting often stem from misunderstandings or mishandling of the composting process.

Once you understand the basics of composting and how to manage your compost pile, you'll realize that composting isn't smelly, doesn't have to attract pests, isn't overly complicated or time-consuming, and doesn't require much space.

Like any new skill, composting comes with a learning curve. But with some patience and practice, you'll soon find composting to be a simple and satisfying way to reduce waste and enhance your garden's health. So, don't let these myths discourage you. Try composting, and you might just discover a new, green hobby.

Seasonal Composting

Composting is a year-round process that changes and adapts to the ebb and flow of the seasons. The environmental conditions - temperature, humidity, rainfall - all affect the composting process's speed and efficiency. As nature takes its course over the year, the process of composting requires some adjustments to maintain its rhythm. Understanding the intricacies of seasonal composting is essential for making the most out of your composting efforts. From the warming days of spring to the chill of winter, each season brings unique considerations for your compost pile. Here we will delve into the specifics of composting during each season, providing you with the knowledge to maintain a thriving compost pile, regardless of the weather outside.

Spring Composting

Spring is a period of rebirth and renewal in nature, and it's no different for your compost pile. As the frost of winter softens, the warming weather wakes up the dormant microbes in your compost pile, leading to a surge in microbial activity and an acceleration in the composting process. This season is perfect for incorporating the fresh green waste your garden will produce—grasses begin to grow more rapidly, annual weeds sprout, and plants require more regular pruning. All these materials are rich in nitrogen, vital for the balanced diet of your compost microbes.

However, with the increased activity comes an increased need for oxygen. This is where turning your compost pile becomes crucial, not just to help aerate and provide the necessary oxygen for aerobic decomposition but also to evenly distribute the heat generated from microbial activity and avoid creating anaerobic conditions that could lead to unpleasant smells. But be mindful, as frequent turning could also lead to quicker drying, which is not ideal for composting. Balance is key.

Summer Composting

In summer, the composting process hits its peak. This is the season when your compost pile may be working at its fastest, turning your organic waste into rich compost more quickly than in other seasons. The warm temperatures and longer daylight hours can significantly enhance the composting process, aiding in rapid decomposition.

However, the heat of summer can also pose challenges. Your compost pile might dry out faster than usual, and maintaining adequate moisture levels becomes critical. A compost pile that's too dry will slow down or halt the decomposition process because the microbes that facilitate the process need moisture to survive. You'll have to monitor the pile closely and add water occasionally to ensure the compost doesn't dry out.

In addition to keeping an eye on moisture, continue to add fresh green waste and turn your compost pile regularly. This season is all about maintenance and ensuring that your compost pile is functioning at its optimum level.

Autumn Composting

As summer fades into autumn, the composting process undergoes a transition. You'll start to see an abundance of brown waste materials in the form of fallen leaves and dead plants—nature's way of providing the carbon needed to balance out the nitrogen-rich green waste from the earlier months. This season gives you the perfect materials to create a balanced compost pile. It's an opportunity to layer in brown materials, which will aid aeration and bulk up your compost pile, preparing it for the cooler months ahead.

This is also an ideal time to give your compost pile a good turn, mixing the green waste from summer with the newly added brown materials. The mixing helps to speed up decomposition by improving aeration and distributing the different materials more evenly, enhancing the overall composting process. Yet, be aware that too many brown materials can slow down decomposition due to their slower breakdown rate and low nitrogen content.

Winter Composting

Winter is often seen as a dormant period for composting, but it doesn't have to be. Although the process slows down due to the cold temperatures, it doesn't stop completely. The core of the compost pile can remain warm, providing a cozy refuge for microbes to continue their work.

During this season, the size of your compost pile matters. A larger pile holds heat far longer than a smaller one, which aids in preserving microbial activity. If your pile is too small, it may freeze solid and halt composting until the weather warms again.

One of the challenges of winter composting is protecting your pile from excessive moisture due to rain or snow. Excessive moisture can create anaerobic conditions and slow down the decomposition process. Adding a layer of insulation, like straw or a compost cover, can help retain warmth, fend off excessive moisture, and keep the composting process alive through the winter.

Understanding the seasonal cycles of composting allows you to better manage your compost pile, ensuring its success regardless of the weather.

Troubleshooting Common Composting Problems

Composting is a natural, organic process that transforms everyday waste into nutrient-rich soil, which is crucial for any garden. However, like any organic system, it's not immune to challenges and occasional hiccups, especially for newbies. Navigating these challenges successfully hinges on understanding their origins and how to remedy them. Maintaining a delicate balance is essential in composting. Missteps can occur, but they don't mean failure. Instead, they're opportunities to learn and adjust your approach, bringing the process back on track.

As you begin composting, remember that you're essentially building a habitat for billions of microscopic organisms. These tireless workers are the magic behind composting, as they break down your kitchen scraps and yard waste. However, these microorganisms are sensitive to their environment, and any deviation from optimal living conditions can cause issues. The good news is that once you understand the root cause, these problems can be remedied relatively easily.

Let's now begin to understand these challenges on a deeper level. By learning their root causes and the effective strategies to address them, we can arm ourselves with the right knowledge to overcome these common issues.

Slow Decomposition

Slow decomposition is a common issue many composters face. This process, primarily driven by the activity of microbes like bacteria and fungi, can be hindered by several factors. Let's break this down in simpler terms and look at the solutions to quicken the decomposition process.

When we say an "imbalance of green and brown materials," we are essentially talking about the nitrogen-to-carbon ratio in your compost pile. Green materials, like vegetable scraps, coffee grounds, or fresh grass clippings, are rich in nitrogen. They provide the protein that microbes need to grow and multiply. Brown materials, such as dry leaves, straws, or shredded newspaper, are high in carbon. Carbon acts as an energy source for the microbes and helps add structure to the compost pile, improving air circulation.

If there's too much nitrogen (too many greens), the compost pile can become overly wet and smelly, and the decomposition process can slow down. Conversely, if there's too much carbon (too many browns), the compost pile can be too dry, and decomposition will also slow down.

Solution: A good rule of thumb is to aim for a balance, generally a 2:1 ratio of browns to greens. This doesn't have to be strict; composting is quite forgiving. But keeping this guideline in mind can help you optimize the decomposition process.

Unbalanced Moisture and Oxygen

The other factors, moisture, and oxygen, are also crucial for composting. Microbes, like all living things, need water to live. But too much water can fill the air spaces in the compost pile and create an environment that favors less desirable, odor-producing microbes. On the other hand, oxygen is needed for the microbes to break down the organic matter. Lack of oxygen can encourage those unwanted microbes, leading to a slow, smelly composting process.

Solution: Keep your compost pile as damp as a wrung-out sponge and turn it every few weeks. This will help distribute moisture evenly and introduce fresh oxygen into the pile, creating an ideal environment for efficient decomposition. Turning the pile can be as simple as mixing it with a pitchfork or composting tool.

Unpleasant Odors

Unpleasant odors often indicate that there is something wrong with your compost pile. Most of the time, it's a sign of two major issues: excessive moisture or poor aeration, both of which pave the way for an overabundance of certain bacteria. Let's discuss them in more detail and address potential solutions.

When your compost pile gets overly wet, it can lead to the overgrowth of anaerobic bacteria. These bacteria thrive in conditions where oxygen is scarce. As a side effect of their metabolic processes, they produce gases that can emit foul odors reminiscent of rotten eggs or garbage. Too much green material, which is rich in moisture, or prolonged exposure to rain, can often lead to an overly wet compost pile.

Conversely, poor aeration can also contribute to the rise of these odor-causing, anaerobic bacteria. Composting is an aerobic process, meaning it needs oxygen. A pile that is too compact or is not turned frequently enough can lack the oxygen necessary for aerobic bacteria to flourish, the types of bacteria we want in our compost as they expedite decomposition and don't produce unpleasant odors.

Solution: Turning your compost pile more frequently helps promote aeration, introduce oxygen back into the pile, and speed up the aerobic decomposition process. A good practice is to turn your compost pile every few weeks.

Adding more brown materials to the pile can be an effective way to absorb excess moisture. Brown materials are high in carbon and are typically dry, providing the dual benefits of soaking up extra water and balancing the carbon-to-nitrogen ratio.

Monitoring the weather and protecting your compost pile during prolonged periods of rain can also prevent your compost from getting overly wet. You can try covering your compost bin or pile during heavy rain or moving your bin under a shelter if possible.

Managing Pests

Managing pests is another significant aspect of successful composting. A poorly maintained compost pile can unwittingly become a breeding ground for a variety of pests. Let's review some common ones and how they interact with your compost.

- Rats and Mice: These small mammals are attracted to food waste, particularly meats, dairy, and cooked food leftovers. They can burrow into a compost pile and even make it their home, creating a potential health risk.

- Flies and Other Insects: These are the most common pests you may encounter. They lay eggs in the compost, leading to an infestation of maggots, which, while helpful in breaking down the compost material, can become a nuisance in large numbers.

- Raccoons: These clever creatures like the smell of food scraps. They can be particularly troublesome as they are adept at opening latches and are known to create quite a mess.

- Ants: Finding ants in your compost pile might indicate that your compost is too dry. Ants are attracted to the sweet smell of kitchen scraps and can become an issue if you allow them to increase.

- Wasps: These insects are attracted to the sweetness of fruit scraps in the compost. While they do not directly harm the composting process, their nests can be a danger to people nearby.

Solution: The key to managing these pests lies mainly in what you put into your compost pile. Avoid composting meat, dairy, and cooked foods, which are particularly attractive to pests. Also, make sure to bury fresh material under a layer of brown materials, such as leaves or straw, which can help mask the odor.

For bin composting systems, double-check that your bin has a tight-fitting lid and, if needed, a latch to keep larger pests like rats and raccoons away. If insects become an issue, consider adding a layer of garden soil or finished compost to the top of your pile, which can deter flies from laying eggs.

Regulate Temperature

Regulating the temperature of your compost pile can be a bit of a balancing act, but it's essential for successful composting. The internal temperature of your compost pile can indicate how effectively the organic materials are being decomposed. Millions of microorganisms carry out this decomposition process, and as they break down the organic material, they generate heat. Let's go through this in detail, including the effects of the temperature and how to effectively regulate it.

The compost pile needs to reach a specific temperature range to efficiently break down the materials and ensure any undesirable elements, such as weed seeds and harmful pathogens, are killed off. Ideally, the core of a compost pile should heat up to between 130 to 160 degrees Fahrenheit (55 to 70 degrees Celsius). This is often called the thermophilic phase of composting, during which thermophilic (heat-loving) bacteria thrive and accelerate decomposition.

However, if the compost pile gets too hot, usually over 170 degrees Fahrenheit (77 degrees Celsius), it can harm the composting process. At these higher temperatures, beneficial microorganisms that aid decomposition can be killed off, and the compost pile can start to dry out, inhibiting the necessary biological activity.

Solution: Regularly monitoring the temperature of your compost pile is crucial if you want your composting to be successful. A compost thermometer, which is a long-stemmed thermometer designed to probe into the center of the pile, is a handy tool for this. These thermometers are designed to resist the heat and humidity of a compost pile, and the long stem allows you to measure the temperature at the pile's core. If the pile becomes too hot, turning the compost can help it cool down. Turning the compost introduces fresh oxygen, essential for aerobic bacteria, and redistributes the materials, which can help lower the temperature. Alternatively, if the compost pile isn't heating up enough, adding more green materials (high in nitrogen) or reducing the size of the compost materials for easier breakdown can help increase the temperature.

Recognizing these common problems and understanding their causes allows you to take the necessary steps to prevent them, ensuring your composting journey is fruitful.

Safety Guidelines

As we begin our exciting journey into the world of composting, we need to discuss first - safety. Now, before you start worrying, let me reassure you. Composting is generally as safe as making a sandwich. Well, a sandwich made from kitchen scraps and yard waste, but still, a sandwich!

However, just like with any new hobby or skill, there are a few things to keep an eye out for to ensure you're composting safely. Just as you wouldn't juggle with sharp knives without learning how to juggle first, we don't want to dive headfirst into composting without understanding the potential risks.

So, let's take some time to talk about safety in composting. Think of it as the seatbelt that keeps you secure on this thrilling composting journey. It won't take the fun out of the ride, but it will help you avoid any unexpected bumps along the way.

Understanding Composting Pathogens

First, let's talk about what pathogens are. The word 'pathogen' might sound like something out of a sci-fi movie, but it's just a fancy term for microorganisms that can cause diseases in humans or animals. Pathogens come in all shapes and sizes, including bacteria, viruses, fungi, and parasites.

Now, you might be wondering, "How do these microscopic party crashers end up in my compost pile?" Well, they hitch a ride on the raw materials you add to your compost. Think about it: kitchen scraps, yard waste, and manure aren't exactly sterile. They can carry a variety of microorganisms, including pathogens.

In a well-managed compost pile, these pathogens don't stick around for long. The composting process involves decomposition, which generates heat, and believe me; most pathogens aren't fans of high temperatures. But, if your compost pile doesn't heat up enough or certain materials aren't properly composted, some pathogens might stick around a bit longer.

Common Pathogens in Compost: E. coli and Salmonella

Let's talk about a couple of the usual suspects regarding pathogens in compost: Escherichia coli (or E. coli, as it's commonly known) and Salmonella. These bacteria are often found in the digestive tracts of humans and animals, and they can end up in compost if you're composting manure or food waste. If ingested, these bacteria can cause unpleasant illnesses, so we definitely don't want them hanging around in our compost.

Conditions that Favor Pathogens and How to Manage Them

So, what kind of environment do these microscopic party crashers like? Well, pathogens are a bit like Goldilocks - they prefer just the right conditions. They love moisture, are not fans of extreme temperatures, and need food to grow. Here's the thing: a compost pile offers all of these, but don't worry, we can manage these conditions to make our compost pile a lot less appealing to pathogens.

Temperature: The composting process generates heat, and most pathogens can't survive high temperatures. In fact, compost piles can get as hot as 140 to 160 degrees Fahrenheit (60 to 70 degrees Celsius) - enough to wipe out most pathogens. To ensure your compost pile heats up properly, you must have a good mix of green (nitrogen-rich) and brown (carbon-rich) materials, keep the compost pile moist but not wet, and turn the pile regularly to let oxygen in.

Moisture: Pathogens love moisture, but they don't like to swim. This means that while your compost pile needs to be moist to facilitate decomposition, it shouldn't be waterlogged. If your compost pile is too wet, it can create an anaerobic (oxygen-free) environment that specific pathogens love. To avoid this, make sure your compost pile has good drainage, and if you're adding a lot of wet materials (like food scraps), balance them out with dry, brown materials (like leaves or straw).

Food: Pathogens need food to grow; certain materials in your compost pile can provide that food. In particular, meat, dairy, and pet waste can harbor pathogens. While these materials can be composted, they require careful management and high temperatures to ensure pathogens are killed off. If you're a beginner composter, it might be best to avoid these materials until you're more comfortable with managing your compost pile.

Safe Composting Practices to Minimize Pathogens

Having discussed the presence of microscopic pathogens, addressing methods for controlling their proliferation is essential. The objective is to create a compost pile that is as unfavorable for pathogen growth as possible.

The Importance of High Temperatures in Compost Piles

The first weapon in our pathogen-busting arsenal is heat. Yes, you heard it right! Your compost pile is not just a nutrient factory but a natural oven that can crank up the heat to levels most pathogens cannot stand.

Remember that composting is a bit like cooking. You need the right ingredients (a mix of greens and browns), the right amount of water (not too much, not too little), and good air circulation (so turn that pile!). When all these factors are in balance, your compost pile will heat up and reach temperatures high enough to send those pathogens packing.

How hot, you ask? You're aiming for temperatures between 130 and 160 degrees Fahrenheit (55 to 70 degrees Celsius). Now, unless you're a superhero with heat vision, you'll need a compost thermometer to keep track of your pile's temperature. Check different parts of the pile, as the temperature can vary throughout.

Handling Pet Waste and Meat/Dairy Products

Next, let's talk about certain types of waste requiring extra care: pet waste, and meat and dairy products. These are like the VIP guests at the pathogen party - they can harbor a lot of pathogens and need to be handled properly.

Pet Waste

If you have a dog or a cat, you might be tempted to toss their poop into your compost pile. After all, it's organic, right? Well, while it's true that pet waste can be composted, it can also contain pathogens that are harmful to humans. So, if you're planning on using your compost in your vegetable garden or anywhere else where it might come into contact with humans, it's best to leave pet waste out. If you really want to compost pet waste, consider having a separate compost pile just for this purpose, and use the resulting compost on ornamental plants, not on your veggie patch.

Meat and Dairy Products

Similar rules apply to meat and dairy products. While it's possible to compost these, they can attract unwanted pests and harbor pathogens if not composted correctly. Generally, avoiding adding these to your compost pile is best, especially if you're new to composting. If you decide to compost meat and dairy, make sure your compost pile is hot enough (remember our chat about temperature?) and that these items are well mixed into the pile to speed up their decomposition and reduce the risk of pests.

Using Gloves and Other Protective Equipment

Lastly, let's talk about gearing up for safety. Just like you wouldn't go into a battle without armor, you shouldn't handle compost without some basic protective gear. The most essential piece of equipment is a good pair of gloves. Gloves protect your hands from pathogens and any sharp or rough materials in your compost pile.

If you're turning your compost pile or spreading compost in your garden, you might also want to consider wearing a dust mask, especially if you're sensitive to dust or have allergies. Compost can release a lot of dust, and you don't want to breathe that in.

And remember, after handling compost, wash your hands thoroughly. It's a simple step, but it's one of the best ways to protect yourself from any potential pathogens.

Physical Safety in Composting

Composting is not just about dealing with microscopic organisms; it's also about ensuring you don't accidentally twist an ankle, strain your back, or cut yourself while managing your compost pile. So, let's dive into some physical safety tips.

Turning Compost Piles: It's All in the Technique

Turning your compost pile is a bit like a workout. It helps to get the oxygen flowing and the decomposition happening, but it also requires some physical effort. If done improperly, you could end up with a sore back or even an injury.

Now, you don't need to be a fitness guru to turn a compost pile, but you do need to use proper technique. Always bend at the knees, not the waist, when lifting compost material, and use your leg muscles, not your back. Keep your movements smooth and controlled, and avoid twisting your body unnecessarily. And remember, it's better to make a few shorter trips than try to move a big heap of compost all at once and strain yourself in the process.

The Right Tools for the Job

Just like a chef needs a good set of knives, a composter needs the right tools. A compost fork or pitchfork is a must-have for turning your compost pile. It's specifically designed for the job and will make it easier and safer.

A good pair of gardening gloves protect your hands from sharp materials, and a wheelbarrow can be a lifesaver when composting around your garden. Remember, using the right tools not only makes composting easier but it also reduces the risk of injury.

Remember the old saying, "A workman is only as good as his tools"? Well, it rings true in composting as well! But there's one more thing we need to discuss: ergonomics.

Ergonomics in Composting: Your Back Will Thank You

Ergonomics might sound like a big fancy word, but it's all about ensuring that the things you do and the tools you use are designed to work with your body, not against it. And trust me; ergonomics is your best friend when it comes to composting.

When you're turning your compost pile, using a compost fork or pitchfork with a long handle can save your back from unnecessary strain. The long handle allows you to stand upright while turning the compost, reducing the need to bend or stoop. And don't forget about lifting - always use your legs, not your back, when lifting heavy loads.

If you're using a compost bin or tumbler, make sure it's at a comfortable height for you. You shouldn't have to reach too high or bend too low to add materials or remove compost. Consider raising your compost bin off the ground or using a step stool if necessary.

Also, remember to take breaks. Composting is a marathon, not a sprint. It's better to take regular short breaks than to push yourself to the point of exhaustion. Listen to your body - if you're tired or something starts to hurt, take a break.

And finally, stay hydrated, especially on hot days. It's easy to lose track of time when you're knee-deep in composting, but remember to take care of yourself too.

Safe Use of Finished Compost

Let's imagine that you've done all the hard work, you've turned and mixed and monitored your compost pile, and now you've got this earthy-smelling finished compost. But hold on a second; before we start spreading it all over the garden, let's talk about how to use finished compost safely.

The Waiting Game: Ensuring Complete Composting

First things first, you want to make sure that your compost is fully "cooked" before you use it. What do I mean by that? Well, composting is a process, and like any good recipe, it takes time to get it just right. If you use compost that's not fully decomposed, you run the risk of introducing pathogens into your garden.

So, how do you know when your compost is ready? Well, finished compost should be dark and crumbly, like rich garden soil. It should smell earthy and pleasant, not rotten or sour. And you shouldn't be able to recognize any of the original materials you put in there (bye-bye, banana peels, and apple cores!).

If you're not sure if your compost is ready, it's better to wait a bit longer. When in doubt, give it another couple of weeks and check again.

A Place for Everything: Using Compost Wisely in the Garden

Once you've got your finished compost, it's time to put it to work in your garden. But where should it go? Well, that depends on what went into your compost pile. If you've been careful to avoid adding potential pathogen sources like meat, dairy, or pet waste, then your compost can go just about anywhere. But if there's a chance that these materials made their way into your compost pile, it's best to play it safe.

Playing it Safe with Edible Crops

If your compost includes materials that could harbor pathogens, avoid using it directly on or around plants that produce the food you'll be eating raw, like lettuce or tomatoes. Instead, use it around non-edible plants or in areas of your garden where you're just looking to improve the soil structure and fertility. Better safe than sorry, right?

Washing Produce: Don't Skip This Step!

One last piece of advice about using compost safely: always wash your produce. Yes, even if it's homegrown and even if you've used the most perfect, well-managed compost in your garden. Washing produce is an essential step to remove any residual soil, which could contain pathogens.

But hey, this isn't a chore; it's a ritual! There's something incredibly satisfying about bringing in a haul of fresh produce from your garden, washing it off, and seeing the vibrant colors of your fruits and veggies shine. Plus, it's a great way to remind yourself of the journey from waste to wealth that your compost—and your garden—have undergone.

In conclusion, composting is an amazing process that transforms kitchen scraps and yard waste into black gold for our gardens. It's a rewarding journey that connects us with nature's cycles and helps us contribute to a healthier planet. However, like any journey, it's important to travel safely.

By understanding and respecting the process, we can manage potential risks and ensure that our composting practices are healthful and beneficial, both for us and for the environment. Remember, it's not just about creating nutrient-rich soil—it's about fostering a greener lifestyle that values sustainability, resourcefulness, and care for our shared environment.

So let's put on our gardening gloves, roll up our sleeves, and get composting. With a little knowledge and a lot of love, we can turn our waste into wealth, improve our gardens, and do our part for the planet. Here's to safe and successful composting!

BOOK III

MASTERING COMPOST TECHNIQUES

ADVANCED STRATEGIES FOR A THRIVING GARDEN

The world of composting isn't a one-size-fits-all process. Just as gardens reflect the individuality of their gardeners, composting techniques can be as diverse and unique as the people employing them. This flexibility is a testament to composting's universal appeal and applicability.

In this book, we will delve into the various composting techniques available to you, each with its own set of advantages, considerations, and distinctive charm. From traditional pile composting to innovative composting machines, worm composting's wriggly wonders, and the low-maintenance allure of trench and sheet composting - there's a composting method for every lifestyle, need, and ambition.

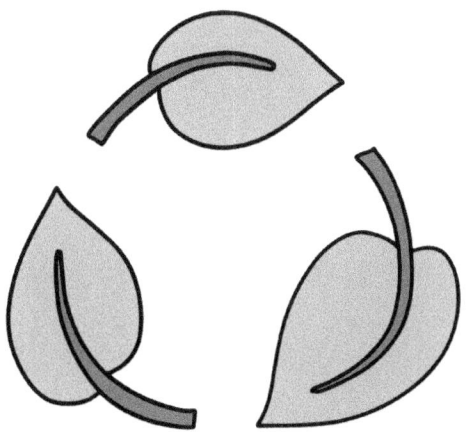

Traditional Composting: An Accessible Method for Every Gardener

B ased on the natural breakdown of organic materials over time, this system has been used for centuries, predating our modern understanding of biology and environmental science. It's a testament to our ancestors' wisdom in managing waste, enhancing soil fertility, and living sustainably.

Bin or pile composting, at its core, is a straightforward process that involves piling organic waste, often in a specifically designated container or bin, and letting nature take its course. Over time, with the help of billions of microscopic decomposers and a few larger helpers like worms and insects, this waste transforms into a rich, soil like substance known as compost, often referred to as "black gold" by gardeners. This transformation is not just waste reduction—it's alchemy on the most practical and beneficial level.

Understanding the suitability and benefits of bin or pile composting can illuminate why this method is so widely practiced. Firstly, it's incredibly adaptable and can be tailored to your specific needs. Whether you have a small urban garden, a suburban backyard, or even a rural homestead, a version of bin or pile composting can work for you.

This method is flexible when it comes to space and volume. A compost pile can be as simple as a heap in the corner of your yard, or you can use a bin that keeps things neat and can fit into smaller spaces. The bin could be a simple repurposed container, a commercially available compost bin with all the bells and whistles, or a DIY construction tailored to your needs.

The benefits of bin or pile composting are manifold. It allows you to recycle a substantial portion of your household waste, reducing your environmental impact and diverting waste from landfill. But perhaps the most tangible benefit appears in your garden. Compost made through this method is a nutrient-dense, soil-enhancing material that can improve plant health, boost crop yields, and help maintain soil moisture levels.

The process also presents a learning opportunity. It's a practical way for adults to understand nature's recycling process and our role within it. For children, it's an engaging, hands-on biology lesson demonstrating nature's cycle of life, decay, and rebirth.

Materials Needed

Composting, at its heart, is a nature-driven process. With the right ingredients and conditions, nature does most of the work for us. As you embark on your composting journey, you will need a few basic tools and materials to create the right environment for this process to flourish. In this section, we'll discuss the types of bins, the suitable organic waste materials, and the tools that can help make your composting experience more efficient and rewarding.

Types of Bins: Bought vs. DIY Options

When choosing a compost bin, there are plenty of options. Some people might opt to purchase a commercially available compost bin. These come in various styles, including stationary, tumbling, and worm bins, each with its own set of benefits. Stationary bins are sturdy and can hold a lot of compost but require you to manually turn the compost. Tumbling bins make turning the compost easier, and worm bins (or vermicomposters) utilize worms to speed up the decomposition process.

On the other hand, if you're feeling handy or are on a budget, you can make a DIY compost bin. Old wooden pallets, wire mesh, or even repurposed trash bins can be converted into functional compost bins. The key features to include in your DIY bin are adequate ventilation for airflow and an accessible way to turn the compost and retrieve the finished product.

Composting Tools: Pitchforks, Aerators, and Thermometers

A few essential tools can make your composting journey easier. A garden fork or pitchfork is essential for turning your compost pile. Regularly turning your compost helps to aerate the pile, speeding up decomposition and reducing odors. An aerator tool, which you push into the pile and then pull out, is another tool that can help increase airflow in the pile.

A compost thermometer can be a helpful tool for those who want to track the progress of their compost pile. Compost piles heat up as the organic materials break down, and a thermometer can help you ensure your pile is at the optimal temperature (between 130 and 160 degrees Fahrenheit).

Setting Up Your Compost Bin (or Pile)

Initiating your composting endeavor involves three crucial steps: choosing the right location, preparing your composting site, and creating a balanced composition of organic materials. This may sound daunting at first, but once you understand these steps, you'll realize it's a simple, straightforward process.

Selecting the Perfect Location

You should consider several factors when deciding on your compost bin or pile location. Firstly, convenience is key. The composting site should be close enough to your house or garden for easy disposal of kitchen scraps and easy access to the finished compost. However, if you're worried about odors (which, if managed properly, should be minimal), you may not want it directly adjacent to living spaces.

Secondly, the site should ideally be level and have good drainage to prevent water from pooling, which could create anaerobic conditions unfavorable for composting. Consider a spot with partial shade; too much sun can dry out the compost pile, while an entirely shaded area may keep it too cool.

Preparing Your Bin or Pile: Starting with Browns

Once you've chosen the location, the next step is to prepare your bin or pile. If you're using a bin, ensure it has holes for aeration and drainage. Starting a compost pile directly on bare earth can allow beneficial organisms from the soil to migrate into the compost more easily, boosting the decomposition process.

Start your compost pile or bin with a layer of browns—these carbon-rich materials like straw, dried leaves, or shredded newspaper provide a good base, enhancing aeration and drainage at the bottom of the pile. Aim for a layer about 4-6 inches deep.

Layering Your Materials: Achieving the Perfect Balance

Following the brown layer, add a layer of green materials—your kitchen scraps like vegetable peelings, coffee grounds, or fresh grass clippings. These nitrogen-rich materials are the "fuel" for the decomposing microorganisms. Try to match the volume of the green layer to that of the brown layer.

Continue to alternate layers of browns and greens. Maintaining this balance helps ensure efficient decomposition, minimizes odors, and results in a healthier compost. If your compost pile becomes too wet or smelly, add more browns. If it's not decomposing quickly enough, add more greens or ensure the pile is moist like a wrung-out sponge.

Setting up your compost pile or bin is like setting the foundation for a house—get it right, and the rest of the process should run smoothly.

Maintaining Your Compost Bin (or Pile)

Once your compost pile or bin is set up, maintaining it requires some care, although the amount of work involved is quite manageable. Regular turning, monitoring moisture and temperature, and troubleshooting common issues are the main tasks to keep your compost healthy and productive.

When and How to Turn Your Compost

Turning your compost is a vital step to ensure efficient decomposition. It helps to aerate the pile, introduces fresh materials to the decomposer organisms, and helps distribute heat evenly. Aim to turn your compost pile or bin every 1-2 weeks.

Use a pitchfork or a compost-turning tool to mix up the layers to turn your compost pile. Try to bring the material from the edges into the center, where it's hottest, and decomposition is most active, and move the central material out to the edges.

Moisture and Temperature Management

Managing moisture and temperature in your compost pile can greatly affect the speed and efficiency of the composting process. Your compost pile should be as damp as a wrung-out sponge. If it's too dry, decomposition will slow down; if it's too wet, it can become smelly and anaerobic.

Adding water or more green materials can help if your compost pile is too dry. If it's too wet, add more browns and ensure your pile has adequate drainage. Turning the pile can also help dry out a too-wet pile.

Temperature-wise, a healthy compost pile can heat up to between 130 and 160 degrees Fahrenheit due to the activity of the decomposer organisms. If your pile is within this range, it's a good sign that decomposition is progressing well. A compost thermometer can be a helpful tool to monitor this.

Troubleshooting Common Issues

At times, you may encounter issues with your compost pile. Here are some common problems and their solutions:

1. Odors: A healthy compost pile should smell earthy. If it smells unpleasant, it's usually a sign of too much moisture or a lack of air. Turn the pile and add more browns to fix this.

2. Pests: Fruit flies, rodents, or other pests are often attracted to compost piles because of kitchen scraps. To avoid this, always cover your green material with a layer of browns, and avoid composting meat or dairy products.

3. Slow Decomposition: If your compost pile isn't breaking down as quickly as you'd like, it may be too dry, lack nitrogen-rich green materials, or be too cold. Adding water, greens, or insulating your pile (for example, by surrounding it with straw bales in cold weather) can help.

Tumblers and Composting Machines

While traditional composting methods have been time-tested and nature-approved, modern technology has introduced innovative ways to turn organic waste into nutrient-rich compost. Enter the compost tumbler and composting machines—your space-saving, odor-controlling, and speedy composting solutions.

Compost tumblers are essentially barrels or drums mounted on a stand and equipped with a mechanism to turn or rotate the compost. This design has a few key advantages over a standard compost pile or bin. Firstly, the turning mechanism makes mixing and aerating the compost easy, promoting faster decomposition. Because all the compost material is enclosed in the tumbler, there's also less risk of attracting pests. Moreover, the composting process tends to be quicker in a tumbler because of the increased aeration and ease of turning.

Composting machines, on the other hand, offer a high-tech solution to composting. These devices range from small kitchen appliances designed for composting a household's daily food waste to larger, more sophisticated machines for commercial or municipal composting. Most composting machines speed up the decomposition process by grinding or shredding the waste, maintaining optimal temperature, and sometimes even introducing specific microorganisms to aid decomposition. The result is a quick and convenient composting process that can take as little as a few hours for small-scale models and up to several weeks for larger ones.

It's important to note that while both compost tumblers and composting machines offer some significant advantages, they might not be the right choice for everyone. These methods are more expensive and less 'natural' than traditional composting methods. They can also have limitations on the types and quantities of waste they can handle. For instance, compost tumblers often have a limited capacity and might not compost large quantities of waste as effectively as a traditional compost pile.

When deciding whether to go the traditional route or opt for a tumbler or composting machine, consider your composting needs, budget, and personal preferences. Whichever path you choose, remember that the core purpose remains the same: transforming waste into a valuable resource and contributing to a more sustainable and circular way of living.

Trench Composting: The Underground Solution

Trench composting is a technique of composting where organic waste material is buried in trenches dug in the ground. It's a straightforward, no-frills method of returning organic matter to the soil, utilizing the natural decomposition process to create a rich, fertile environment in which plants will thrive.

Unlike other composting methods that require a specific bin or a pile, trench composting occurs right where your garden is. By burying the compost materials directly in the soil, you're creating a nutrient-rich zone for plant roots to help ensure healthier, more robust plants. This technique is handy for those with limited space or who want to improve the soil quality in specific areas of their garden.

Brief History of Trench Composting

Trench composting is as old as agriculture itself. The earliest farmers understood the cycle of life and death in nature and sought to mimic this process in their fields to ensure a bountiful harvest. They would dig trenches and fill them with plant and animal waste, allowing nature to do the rest.

As societies evolved and agricultural practices refined, so did composting methods. However, trench composting maintained its appeal due to its simplicity and effectiveness. It has been practiced for centuries by many cultures around the world, from the resourceful indigenous tribes in the Americas to the keen gardeners of Victorian England. This technique has stood the test of time, being passed down through generations of gardeners and farmers as a natural, cost-effective, and sustainable way of enriching the soil.

Why Consider Trench Composting?

There are several compelling reasons to consider trench composting. Firstly, it's a relatively simple and hands-off method. Once you've dug your trench and added your organic materials, nature largely takes care of the rest. This makes it an excellent option for beginners who may be intimidated by the perceived complexity of other composting techniques.

Secondly, trench composting is an excellent method for dealing with kitchen waste, leaves, and other compostable materials in an eco-friendly manner. By returning this organic matter to the soil, you're reducing the amount of waste that goes to the landfill and, simultaneously, creating a natural, nutrient-rich supplement for your garden.

Thirdly, trench composting can vastly improve your soil's health over time. The decomposing organic matter enhances soil fertility, improves water retention, and encourages beneficial microbial activity. It's like creating a gourmet buffet for your plants' roots right below the surface.

Finally, if space is an issue, trench composting can be a great solution. There's no need for a compost pile or bin, and you're not sacrificing any garden space since the composting area will also be a planting area.

In conclusion, if you're a gardening novice wanting a simple, sustainable, and space-efficient method to recycle your kitchen waste and enhance your garden's productivity, trench composting could be just what you're looking for.

Materials Needed

Tools for Digging and Covering

The beauty of trench composting lies in its simplicity, and the tools required reflect this. To start trench composting, you'll need some basic gardening tools:

1. *A garden spade or shovel:* You'll use this to dig your composting trench. Depending on the size of your garden or the amount of compostable material you have, the size of the trench can vary. A good starting point is a trench that's about one foot wide, one foot deep, and as long as you need it to be.

2. *A garden fork:* This can be helpful to loosen the soil at the bottom of the trench, which can improve aeration and water drainage. It's also great for mixing the compost materials once they are in the trench.

3. *A wheelbarrow or garden cart:* While not strictly necessary, this can be handy if you have a large amount of compost material to transport to your trench.

4. *A rake or hoe:* You'll use this to cover the compost materials once you've added them to the trench.

Optional Additives

While not necessary for composting, some gardeners use compost activators to kickstart decomposition. These products usually contain a blend of microorganisms and nutrients designed to accelerate composting. You can purchase commercial compost activators or make your own by adding a few shovelfuls of finished compost or garden soil (full of beneficial microorganisms) to your trench.

Remember that the key to successful trench composting, or any composting, lies in balancing your inputs. Strive for a good mix of green (nitrogen-rich) and brown (carbon-rich) materials, add a bit of moisture if needed, and let nature do the rest!

Step-by-step Guide to Trench Composting

1. Choosing the Right Location for Your Trench

The first step in the trench composting process involves deciding where to place your trench. Ideally, you want a convenient location for your kitchen scraps and garden waste. If you have a specific area in your garden where you'd like to boost fertility, such as a future vegetable bed or a perennial border, this could be a great spot for your trench. Remember, you'll be planting directly into this nutrient-rich soil once the composting process is complete.

Remember that composting is a process of decay, which can attract pests. Hence, you might want to avoid places directly next to your home. Also, avoid areas where water tends to pool in your garden, as you want your compost trench to drain well and not become waterlogged.

2. Preparing the Trench: Depth, Width, Length

Grab your trusty spade or shovel, it's time to dig your compost trench. The dimensions of your trench can vary depending on the amount of compostable material you have and the space you have available. As a general guideline, aim for a trench about one foot wide and one foot deep. The length of the trench can vary, but it's often convenient to make it a manageable length, such as the width of a garden bed.

Once you've dug your trench, consider using a garden fork to loosen the soil at the bottom. This is not essential but can improve the drainage and aeration of the composting materials, helping to speed up the composting process.

3. Layering Your Materials: A Guide to Green and Brown Layers

Now comes the fun part: adding your composting materials! The goal is to create a balanced mix of 'greens' and 'browns'. 'Greens' are nitrogen-rich materials like fruit and vegetable scraps, coffee grounds, and fresh grass clippings, while 'browns' are carbon-rich materials like dried leaves, straw, and shredded newspaper.

Start with a layer of browns at the bottom of the trench. This will help with aeration and drainage. Then add a layer of greens, followed by another layer of browns. Aim for a roughly equal mix of greens and browns by volume, but don't worry if it's imperfect. The beauty of trench composting is that it's a very forgiving process. Nature is good at balancing things out!

4. Closing and Marking the Trench

Once you've filled your trench with composting materials, it's time to close it up. Use your spade or shovel to backfill the trench with the soil you removed when digging. Try to mound the soil slightly above ground level, as it will settle over time. Then pat the soil down gently with the back of your spade or rake.

Next, mark the location of your trench. You could use a plant marker, a string line, or even a row of stones. This is particularly important if you have several composting trenches in your garden or plan to dig more trenches. The last thing you want is to accidentally dig into a trench that's not fully composted yet!

5. Frequency of Turning the Compost, If Necessary

One of the great benefits of trench composting is that it's a largely 'set it and forget it' method. Unlike some other composting methods, you generally don't need to turn or aerate the compost once it's in the trench. Nature and gravity do most of the work! However, if you notice that decomposition seems to be going very slowly, you could turn the compost to introduce more oxygen and speed up the process. Use a garden fork to gently lift and turn the composting materials, then refill the trench with the soil.

Here are a few things to remember, though:

- Be patient: Trench composting isn't a quick process. Depending on the materials you've used and the climate where you live, it can take anywhere from a few months to a year for the composting process to be complete.

- Be observant: Keep an eye on your compost trench, mainly if it's near plantings. If plants near your compost trench seem to be struggling, it could be a sign that the composting process is drawing too much nitrogen from the soil. In this case, adding a layer of finished compost or sprinkling nitrogen-rich fertilizer around the plants can help.

- Be creative: Don't be afraid to experiment a bit with your trench composting. Try different mixes of greens and browns, adjust the depth of your trench, or add other compost activators. Every garden is unique, and you may find that specific tweaks work particularly well in your situation.

Composting Time Frame

The decomposition time in trench composting can vary significantly depending on the type of organic materials you're using, the local climate, and the specifics of your trench (depth, moisture level, etc.). As a general rule of thumb, most kitchen scraps and garden waste should decompose within a few months to a year.

However, some materials take longer to decompose than others. For example, leaves and grass clippings break down relatively quickly, often within a couple of months. In contrast, tougher, woody materials like small branches or corn cobs can decompose a year or more.

It's important to remember that these time frames are approximations. Composting is a natural process governed by many variables and can be unpredictable. The best approach is to be patient and let nature take its course.

Checking the Readiness of Compost

When your compost is ready, it will be dark, crumbly, and smell like fresh earth. There should be no recognizable pieces of the original materials, except perhaps for a few bits of woody material or hard seeds.

A straightforward way to check if your compost is ready is to dig into the trench with a trowel or garden fork. If you find dark, crumbly material that smells good, your compost is likely ready.

Alternatively, you can take a handful of the compost material and put it in a sealed plastic bag. Let it sit overnight, and then smell it in the morning. If it smells sour or rotten, the compost is not yet finished. But if it smells like fresh earth, it's ready to go!

Precautions When Using Unfinished Compost

While the anticipation of using your homemade compost can be great, waiting until it's fully decomposed before using it around your plants is essential. Unfinished compost can have several negative effects on your garden:

1. Nitrogen theft: As organic material breaks down, it requires nitrogen. If decomposition happens in your garden beds, it may pull nitrogen away from your plants to aid the process, leaving your plants deficient.

2. Disease and pests: Unfinished compost can harbor diseases or pests. Until the composting process is complete, pathogens or pest eggs may not have been sufficiently broken down or outcompeted by beneficial organisms.

3. Phytotoxicity: Some organic materials can release compounds harmful to plants as they break down. These compounds are typically neutralized during the composting process, but if the compost is not fully mature, they could still be present and harm your plants.

4. Weed seeds: Composting generates heat that's intended to kill weed seeds. If the compost hasn't fully matured, some weed seeds may survive and sprout in your garden beds.

Therefore, it's best to let your compost fully mature before using it in your garden to avoid these potential issues. Remember, patience pays off when it comes to composting.

Vermicomposting: Harnessing the Power of Worms

V ermicomposting is a type of composting in which certain species of earthworms are used to enhance the process of organic waste conversion and produce a better end-product. The term "vermi" is Latin for worm, giving us the word vermicomposting, or literally, composting with worms.

The process involves using worms and microorganisms to turn kitchen scraps and other organic waste into a rich, dark, crumbly substance that improves soil health and fertility. Worms consume organic waste and excrete castings, a rich material more commonly referred to as worm poop. These castings are a valuable soil amendment, packed with nutrients readily available for plant uptake.

Vermicomposting is highly beneficial, primarily because it creates a nutrient-dense compost. This compost, known as vermicompost, is incredibly beneficial for soil health, improving plant growth and productivity.

Understanding the Role of Worms in Composting

Worms serve a pivotal function in the composting process, as they assist in converting organic matter into a nutrient-dense compost substance. Here's how they contribute:

1. Digestion and Nutrient Cycling: Worms consume organic waste and transform it into nutrient-rich worm castings (worm poop). They grind the food in their gizzard

as they feed, breaking it down into smaller particles. This process makes nutrients more accessible to plants when the compost is used as a soil amendment.

2. Accelerating Decomposition: The digestion process of worms is quite efficient. They can eat up to their body weight in organic material daily, significantly accelerating decomposition. The resulting vermicompost is ready much faster than compost produced by traditional methods.

3. Improving Soil Structure: As worms move through the compost, they create channels that improve aeration and drainage. This helps prevent the compost from becoming waterlogged and anaerobic, slowing down the composting process and leading to unpleasant odors.

4. Disease Suppression: Research has shown that vermicompost can help suppress plant diseases and pests. This is believed to be due to beneficial microbes introduced and nurtured by the worms in the compost, which can outcompete disease-causing organisms.

So, in the grand scheme of composting, worms are like tiny, efficient compost factories, breaking down waste, cycling nutrients, and improving the overall quality of the compost, making it a valuable addition to any garden or growing environment.

Types of Worms Used in Vermicomposting

When it comes to vermicomposting, not all worms are created equal. Certain species are better suited to the composting environment, with the most popular choices being the Red Wigglers (Eisenia fetida) and European Nightcrawlers (Eisenia hortensis).

- Red Wigglers are often the top choice for vermicomposting. They thrive in decomposing vegetation, are very adaptable to varying environments, and reproduce quickly. Plus, they are voracious eaters, consuming as much as half their body weight in food per day, which makes them perfect for quickly turning your kitchen scraps into nutrient-rich compost.

- European Nightcrawlers, on the other hand, are larger worms and can tolerate cooler temperatures than Red Wigglers. They're known for their ability to break down tougher organic materials thanks to their larger size and stronger muscles.

Although the most commonly used worms are red wigglers (Eisenia fetida) and European nightcrawlers (Eisenia hortensis), other species can also be used effectively:

- African Nightcrawlers (Eudrilus eugeniae): These worms are larger and more temperature resistant than red wigglers, making them ideal for composting in tropical and subtropical climates. They are, however, more vulnerable to cold temperatures.

- Indian Blue Worms (Perionyx excavatus): These worms are fast composters and breed quickly. Similarly, they can adapt to higher temperatures, but they may be more sensitive to environmental changes than other species.

- Alabama Jumpers (Amynthas gracilis): Known for their ability to burrow through hard clay soil, these worms are often used for soil improvement. While they can be used for vermicomposting, they are not as efficient as red wigglers or European nightcrawlers.

The type of worm you choose should depend on your local climate conditions, the amount of waste you produce, and the specific goals you have for your composting project.

Setting Up a Simple Worm Composting System

1. Choose the Right Bin: Worm bins can be made from a variety of materials, but plastic storage containers are often the most convenient and readily available. The size of the bin will depend on the amount of waste you generate, but as a guide, a bin around 10 to 14 inches deep, and about 2x2 feet wide, is a good start for a household.

WORM COMPOSTING

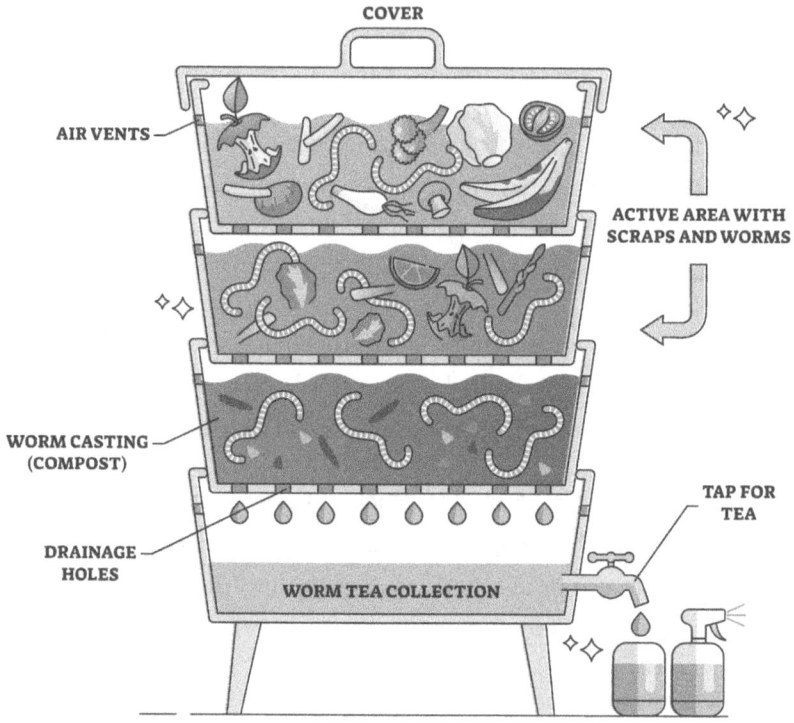

COVER

AIR VENTS

ACTIVE AREA WITH
SCRAPS AND WORMS

WORM CASTING
(COMPOST)

TAP FOR
TEA

DRAINAGE
HOLES

WORM TEA COLLECTION

2. Prepare Your Bin: Drill about 10-15 small holes (around 1/8 to 1/4 inch in diameter) in the bottom for drainage. Also drill some holes around the upper sides of the bin for ventilation - worms need air to survive.

3. Create a Comfortable Environment for Your Worms: To keep your worms happy, think of the tale of Goldilocks - the conditions need to be just right. Aim for a temperature between 55-77°F (13-25°C), which is ideal for most composting worms. They prefer a moist environment - about the same dampness as a wrung-out sponge. Too much water can suffocate the worms, as they breathe through their

skin. Lastly, strive for a near-neutral pH environment. Avoid adding very acidic or alkaline substances.

4. Prepare Bedding for Your Worms: Shredded newspaper, cardboard, or coconut coir makes excellent bedding. This bedding will serve as a home for your worms and eventually break down into compost. Dampen it slightly before adding it to the bin - remember the wrung-out sponge level of wetness.

5. Introduce Your Worms: Purchase composting worms (red wigglers are a popular choice) from a reputable supplier. Add them to the bin and let them burrow into the bedding on their own.

6. Feed Your Worms: Start by adding small amounts of kitchen scraps - vegetable peelings, coffee grounds, or eggshells are all good choices. Avoid meat, dairy, and oily foods, which can attract pests. Bury the scraps under the bedding in one corner of the bin to discourage flies and odors.

7. Cover the Bin: Place a cover over the bin to keep out light (which worms dislike) and to help maintain moisture and temperature levels. This can be as simple as a piece of cardboard or a dark plastic sheet.

8. Create Drainage and Collection System: Place your bin on a couple of bricks or wooden blocks inside a large tray or another bin to catch the liquid that drains out, known as "worm tea". If you want to get sophisticated, you can add a spigot tap to the lower container to make the worm tea easier to collect and use as a liquid fertilizer.

9. Monitor and Maintain Your System: Check the bin regularly to make sure it stays damp and doesn't overheat. Feed the worms gradually, moving around the bin to create new "active areas" and giving them time to fully compost the scraps.

10. Harvest Your Compost: After about 3-4 months, you should find rich, dark compost (worm castings) in the bottom of your bin. You can harvest this and add it directly to your plants - they'll love it!

Remember, worms are living creatures and need to be cared for. The key to successful vermicomposting is to maintain a healthy, comfortable environment for the worms with the right balance of food, moisture, and air.

Feeding Your Worms

Feeding your worms properly is critical for successful vermicomposting. It's like being the head chef in a kitchen for worms and understanding their dietary needs.

What Worms Can Eat

A worm bin is an incredibly powerful and efficient recycling station, converting a diverse range of organic materials into nutrient-rich compost, known as worm castings. Worms, especially red wigglers, can remarkably consume and break down organic waste.

Consider the diet of these worms, which is filled with the scraps of our daily life that we might typically discard. For instance, the worms find fruit and vegetable scraps particularly delectable. Apple cores, carrot peelings, and wilted lettuce could all be turned into a feast for your worms instead of being thrown away.

Yet, the diet of a composting worm goes beyond just fruits and vegetables. They also enjoy coffee grounds, tea bags, and leftovers from our morning rituals, adding more diversity to their meals. Crushed eggshells can also be added to their menu. Besides providing additional nutrients, the calcium in the eggshells helps neutralize any acidity in the bin, maintaining a balanced environment for the worms.

Even materials like non-glossy paper and cardboard find a place in the worm bin. Before being added, these should be shredded and soaked in water to facilitate the worms' ability to consume them. Essentially, you're providing pre-processed food for your worms, making it easier for them to break it down.

Worms can also decompose unusual materials such as hair, fur, and even 100% cotton thread or fabric. These materials degrade over time, and worms aid in this process. However, it's important to know that larger items should be torn or chopped into smaller pieces, not necessarily because the worms can't handle larger pieces but because worms feed on the microorganisms that break down the waste, not the waste itself. So, the smaller the pieces, the greater the surface area for the microorganisms to work on and the quicker the decomposition process.

What to Avoid

Certain wastes could disrupt the bin's harmony or even prove harmful. For example, dairy products and meat or fish wastes are NOT appropriate for a worm bin. As these items decompose, they can give off an unpleasant odor and potentially lure flies and other pests to your bin. Maintaining an odor-free, pest-free composting system thus necessitates careful waste selection.

Likewise, oily or spicy foods should be set aside from the worm bin contents. Worms breathe through their skin, and oily foods could clog their skin pores. Moreover, spicy foods, such as chili peppers, contain capsaicin, which is not worm-friendly.

Certain organic items also warrant exclusion due to their high acidity levels. Although natural, citrus peels and onions can make the worm habitat acidic, causing discomfort to the worms and hindering the composting process.

In the context of yard waste, caution is advised. Plant materials treated with pesticides or herbicides can introduce harmful or lethal chemicals to your worms. Even when the worms survive exposure, these chemicals can throw the worm bin ecosystem off balance.

How Often to Feed the Worms

Feeding your worms is a delicate balance that requires careful observation and understanding of your worm population. The frequency with which you add new organic matter to your worm bin depends on several factors, including the size of your worm population and the rate at which they consume the food scraps.

As a general guideline, you may consider adding new food once the majority of the previous batch of scraps has been consumed. For many worm bin systems, this process usually takes around a week. However, this rate can vary based on the conditions within your bin, such as temperature and moisture level and the type of food scraps you're providing.

Balancing the types of materials you add is vital to maintaining a healthy composting system. When feeding your worms, it's not just about providing food scraps. After each feeding, consider adding a layer of brown materials like shredded newspaper or dried leaves. These carbon-rich elements serve to balance the nitrogen-rich food scraps in the bin while regulating the moisture level. Too much nitrogen can lead to a slimy, smelly compost pile, while a good balance of carbon and nitrogen promotes healthy, odor-free decomposition.

Also, you must avoid overfeeding your worms. While providing them with plenty of food might seem like a good idea, overfeeding can cause issues. Excess food can decompose faster than the worms can consume it, leading to unpleasant odors and potentially attracting pests.

To prevent this, start with smaller quantities of food, gradually increasing the amount as you understand the eating patterns of your worms.

Harvesting Worm Compost

The anticipation of harvesting worm compost is akin to a gardener waiting for the perfect time to pick ripe fruits. It's an art in itself, and understanding when and how to do it is crucial.

Signs the Compost is Ready to Harvest

There are several indicators to tell you that your worm compost is ready for harvesting:

- The compost is dark brown in color, resembling the look of rich, fertile soil.

- It has a crumbly texture, similar to that of a well-done chocolate cake.

- The compost carries a pleasant earthy smell.

- You can see little to no recognizable food or bedding in the bin.

Typically, the compost takes about 2-3 months to reach this stage.

Methods to Harvest Worm Compost

There are a few ways to harvest worm compost. One method is the 'dump and sort' technique, where you empty the entire contents of your bin onto a large sheet and manually separate the worms from the compost. Since worms naturally shy away from light, they will burrow down, allowing you to slowly remove the compost from the top.

Another technique is the 'migration' method. You add fresh bedding and food to only one side of the bin. Over time, the worms will migrate toward the food, leaving you free to harvest the compost from the other side.

Using Worm Compost in Your Garden

Worm compost, often referred to as black gold, is a nutrient-rich soil enhancer. Its high nutrient content can dramatically boost plant growth and enhance soil structure, making it a treasure trove for any gardener. It may be used in a variety of ways in the garden, from top-dressing garden beds and mixing it into potting soil to preparing compost tea to water your plants.

Vermicomposting Troubleshooting

Vermicomposting is a great way to compost food scraps and other organic waste using worms. However, some common problems can arise when implementing this method. Here are a few tips for identifying and solving these issues:

- Odor Issues: A well-maintained worm bin should have a fresh, earthy smell. If an unpleasant odor emanates from your bin, it's usually a sign of excessive moisture or inadequate aeration. If this happens, halt the addition of food scraps for a while. Add dry bedding materials like shredded newspaper or dried leaves to soak up excess moisture. You can improve aeration by turning the compost gently with a hand tool, but be careful not to harm the worms. If your bin doesn't already have aeration holes, consider making some to ensure a good oxygen flow, which is critical for composting organisms.

- Pest Intrusion: Unwanted visitors like fruit flies or mites can infest your worm bin occasionally. Burying food scraps in the bedding material can help deter these pests, as can refraining from overloading the bin with food. In case of a significant pest issue, consider using diatomaceous earth, a natural powder made from tiny fossilized aquatic organisms, which can help control pests without harming the worms.

- Worm Escape Attempts: Your worms are trying to tell you something if you find them crawling up the sides of the bin. Usually, it signifies unfavorable living conditions. Check the moisture levels - the bedding should be as damp as a wrung-out sponge. Acidic foods like citrus fruits or onions can also cause discomfort for the worms, so try to exclude these from your waste input. If you suspect overcrowding is the issue, consider adding more bedding material or splitting the colony into two bins.

Bokashi Composting: Fermentation as a Path to Fertility

Bokashi composting is a unique and efficient method of breaking down organic waste through anaerobic fermentation. Unlike traditional composting, which relies mainly on aerobic decomposition, Bokashi employs the use of beneficial microorganisms that thrive in oxygen-free environments. This method can break down a wide range of organic materials, including those typically not recommended for traditional composting, such as cooked foods, meat, and dairy.

The word "Bokashi" has Japanese origins and translates to "fermented organic matter." Bokashi composting, developed in Japan in the 1980s, is based on ancient techniques of fermenting food waste to produce nutrient-rich soil fertilizers. Dr. Teruo Higa, a professor at the University of Ryukyus in Okinawa, refined and popularized the modern Bokashi composting method by introducing a mix of microorganisms known as Effective Microorganisms (EM). These microorganisms work harmoniously, converting organic waste into a highly fertile soil amendment.

Bokashi composting's unique approach to waste management has gained global popularity for its simplicity, effectiveness, and ability to reduce the environmental impact of waste. The method can be easily adopted by households, schools, and businesses, making it an excellent option for those looking for an eco-friendly waste management solution.

Understanding the Bokashi Process

At the core of the Bokashi composting method is fermentation, an age-old process utilized by various cultures for food preservation. In Bokashi composting, fermentation is essential in breaking down organic matter in an oxygen-deprived environment.

The process starts with the layering of kitchen waste in a Bokashi bin. Each layer of waste is then sprinkled with Bokashi bran, a mixture of wheat bran, molasses, and a community of microorganisms known as Effective Microorganisms (EM), which are the star players in the Bokashi process, working diligently to ferment and break down the organic material without needing oxygen. The result of this fermentation process is a pre-compost material that can be further decomposed in soil or a traditional compost pile.

This is where Bokashi composting markedly diverges from traditional composting. Traditional composting is an aerobic process, meaning it requires oxygen to work effectively. The microorganisms in a traditional compost pile are different species that thrive in oxygen-rich environments. These microbes slowly decompose organic waste, transforming it into a nutrient-rich soil fertilizer.

In contrast, Bokashi composting is an anaerobic or oxygen-free process. It's faster than traditional composting, can handle an extensive array of waste materials, and is basically odor-free. Furthermore, due to its enclosed, compact design, Bokashi composting can be done indoors, making it an excellent option for those with limited outdoor space. It's a fundamentally different yet complementary approach to managing organic waste and improving soil health.

Setting Up a Bokashi Bin

Starting a Bokashi composting journey is a fascinating adventure. First off, let's gather the essential materials and navigate the steps to setting up your Bokashi bin.

Materials Needed

- Bokashi Bin: This is a special compost bin designed for Bokashi composting. It's usually a small, sealed bucket with a tight-fitting lid and a spigot near the bottom to drain off the liquid that forms during fermentation.

- Bokashi Bran: This is a mixture of bran, molasses, and Effective Microorganisms (EM) that kick starts the fermentation process. It's available in many garden stores or online, or you can make your own. [It is a rewarding step on your composting journey. Start with wheat or rice bran as your base, then add Effective Microorganisms (EM), usually available online or at garden stores. These EM are vital as they break down organic material during the Bokashi process. For the EM to thrive, they need food, which is provided by molasses. Then, mix in non-chlorinated water to maintain a healthy environment for the microbes. Combine these ingredients to achieve a damp mixture, spread it out to dry for a few weeks, and you'll have your own Bokashi bran ready for use.]

- Kitchen Scraps: Any organic kitchen waste can be used. This includes fruit and vegetable scraps, coffee grounds, tea bags, and even items like meat and dairy, which are typically not recommended for aerobic composting.

Your Step-by-Step Guide

1. Start with a layer of Bokashi Bran: Start by adding a small layer of Bokashi bran at the bottom of the bin. This will ensure that the composting process starts immediately once the organic material is added.

2. Add Your Kitchen Scraps: Add your organic waste on top of the bran. It's best to cut or break up larger pieces to speed up the composting process.

3. Sprinkle More Bran: Once you've added a layer of waste, sprinkle more Bokashi bran over the top. You're aiming for a light covering over all the waste.

4. Press Down: Compact the waste to eliminate any air pockets since oxygen is not a friend of the Bokashi process; the less air in the bin, the better.

5. Seal the Bin: Close the bin tightly after each addition of waste. Remember, the Bokashi process is anaerobic, so keeping the bin sealed is essential.

6. Repeat: Continue this process until your bin is full.

7. Wait: Once your bin is full, let it sit sealed for two weeks to allow the fermentation process to complete. During this time, drain off the Bokashi juice every few days using the spigot. This liquid can be diluted and used as a plant fertilizer.

Once the two weeks are up, your Bokashi pre-compost is ready. It can be added to a traditional compost pile to finish decomposing, buried in the ground, or mixed into garden soil to improve its fertility.

Using Bokashi Bran

Bokashi bran is the magical ingredient that sets the stage for the Bokashi composting method. But what is it exactly, and how does it catalyze the composting process?

At its heart, Bokashi bran is a carrier medium for a specialized group of microorganisms known as Effective Microorganisms (EM). This bran is typically wheat or rice bran that's been inoculated with a cocktail of beneficial bacteria, yeasts, and fungi. The microorganisms in Bokashi bran are the heroes of the Bokashi composting process, fermenting the organic material in the bin and turning it into nutrient-rich compost.

The role of Bokashi bran is pivotal. It acts as the initiator and accelerator of the fermentation process. When sprinkled on the organic waste in your Bokashi bin, it works by rapidly increasing the population of beneficial microorganisms, which ferment the organic matter, suppresses pathogens, and prevent rotting and foul odors.

The good thing about Bokashi bran is that it's effortless to use. Now, how do we wield this powerful tool effectively? Here's how:

1. Start Strong: Begin with a layer of Bokashi bran at the bottom of your bin. This provides a rich microbial base for your composting journey.

2. Cover Your Scraps: Every time you add a layer of kitchen scraps to your Bokashi bin, cover it with a layer of Bokashi bran. There's no exact measurement required; a light, even sprinkle, should suffice.

3. Seal It Up: Close your bin tightly after each addition, for we want to create an anaerobic—that is, oxygen-free—environment where our fermenting friends can flourish.

4. Drain Regularly: As fermentation progresses, you'll notice a liquid (Bokashi juice) accumulating at the bottom of your bin. Remember to drain this off every few days. It's a potent plant fertilizer when diluted with water.

5. Wait Patiently: Once your bin is full, let it sit sealed for about two weeks. During this time, the microorganisms in the Bokashi bran will do their magic, fermenting the organic waste and transforming it into a pre-compost material.

Feeding Your Bokashi Bin

Feeding your Bokashi bin is a little like feeding a pet: You've got to know its likes and dislikes and how much to feed it to keep it happy and healthy. But don't worry, the rules aren't too strict, and once you get the hang of it, it's as easy as pie.

First, let's talk about the diet of your Bokashi bin. Unlike traditional composting systems, Bokashi composting is an anaerobic process that can handle a broader spectrum of kitchen waste. All your vegetable and fruit scraps, as are cooked foods, dairy products, and even small amounts of meat and fish, are welcome. The microorganisms in the Bokashi bran are pretty voracious and will happily ferment most organic kitchen waste you give them.

However, there are a few things you should avoid putting in your Bokashi bin. Large bones won't break down in the bin and can create an unpleasant smell. Likewise, excessive amounts of liquid, like soups or sauces, can make the compost too wet and disrupt the balance in the bin.

Now, how often should you be adding waste to your bin? The answer is: it depends. The Bokashi composting process is flexible and can adapt to your kitchen waste production. Ideally, you want to add waste to your bin every day or two, but if you produce less waste, it's okay to add it less frequently. Just remember, every time you add waste, you should sprinkle it with a layer of Bokashi bran to start the fermentation process.

Once your Bokashi bin is full, it's time to let the microorganisms do their work. Seal the bin and let it sit undisturbed for about two weeks. During this time, the magic of fermentation will transform your kitchen waste into a nutrient-rich pre-compost.

Harvesting and Using Bokashi Compost

The process of harvesting Bokashi compost is an opportunity to train patience and anticipation. After about two weeks of fermentation, when your compost emits a sweet-sour scent similar to pickles or cider vinegar and there is a white mold-like substance on the surface, you can consider your Bokashi compost ready for harvesting. This white layer is a sign of beneficial microorganisms working their magic.

When it comes to utilizing your freshly harvested Bokashi compost, here are some helpful tips:

1. Let it Mellow: Fresh Bokashi compost is typically acidic. Before planting directly into it, allow it to mellow by integrating it into the soil and waiting about 2-4 weeks.

2. Dig a Trench: A practical way to introduce Bokashi compost to your garden is by digging a trench, adding the compost, and then covering it with about 6-8 inches of soil. This technique allows the compost to blend naturally with the soil.

3. Use in Potted Plants: If you don't have a garden, you can mix Bokashi compost with potting soil to provide nutrient-rich soil for your indoor plants.

4. Share the Wealth: If you have extra Bokashi compost, you can share it with friends, neighbors, or community gardens. It's a wonderful way to contribute to the health of other gardens and foster a sense of community.

5. Start a Composting Project: For those without garden space, consider initiating a community composting project. It's a fantastic way to reduce waste and enrich local green spaces.

Benefits and Challenges of Bokashi Composting

Bokashi composting is a unique practice that comes with a host of benefits. One of the standout advantages of Bokashi composting is its impressive efficiency. Unlike traditional composting, which relies primarily on the slow breakdown of organic materials, Bokashi composting rapidly ferments waste, accelerating the composting process dramatically. While it takes months for traditional composting, in the

Bokashi method, in just a few short weeks, your organic waste is transformed into a nutrient-dense soil fertilizer ready to invigorate your garden.

But it's not just about speed. Bokashi composting boasts a versatile dietary palate, handling an array of organic waste that traditional composting methods might balk at. This includes cooked food, dairy products, and even meat. The ability to break down such a diverse range of materials means less waste ends up in landfills. In addition, it allows you to make the most out of all your kitchen scraps, increasing the nutritional profile of your resulting compost.

For those grappling with space constraints, Bokashi composting offers a valuable solution. Unlike traditional compost piles that require ample backyard space, Bokashi composting operates within a compact bin that could easily fit into a small apartment, balcony, or garage. This spatial efficiency makes composting an accessible option for individuals who live in densely populated urban environments.

Also, those of us who've experienced traditional composting may remember the characteristic odor, an often earthy smell that can be unpleasant if the compost pile is poorly maintained. Thanks to its unique fermentation process, Bokashi composting circumvents this issue entirely. The fermentation process is essentially odor-free, with any smell likened to that of pickles or cider vinegar, making it a less invasive method for composting within your living space.

As with any process, Bokashi composting has its challenges. One of the main ones is sourcing Bokashi bran, which is essential for composting. It can be bought online, which adds an ongoing cost to the process. Alternatively, you can make it yourself, which is a bit time-consuming.

Another challenge is the need for a two-step process. After the fermentation process in the Bokashi bin, the compost needs to be buried in the soil or added to a traditional compost pile to finish the composting process, which could be a challenge for those without access to outdoor space.

Despite these challenges, there are ways to overcome them. Homemade Bokashi bran can be a fun DIY project, or you could pool resources with friends or neighbors to purchase in bulk and reduce costs. As for the two-step process, consider sharing or donating your Bokashi pre-compost to a friend or community garden if you don't have the space to finish the process yourself.

Ultimately, the benefits of Bokashi composting—its speed, efficiency, and wide range of compostable materials—often outweigh the challenges, making it a great composting option for many people.

Grasscycling: A Simple Path to a Healthier Lawn and Planet

Welcome to the world of grasscycling, an eco-friendly practice that simplifies your lawn care routine and provides numerous benefits for the soil and the environment. If you've ever mowed a lawn, you might be familiar with the chore afterward: raking up the grass clippings. Many people bag these clippings and leave them for curbside pickup, not realizing they're discarding a goldmine of natural nutrients. This is where grasscycling enters the picture.

So, what exactly is grasscycling? The term itself is a blend of 'grass' and 'recycling,' and it's precisely that. Grasscycling is the practice of leaving grass clippings on your lawn after mowing instead of bagging them up and sending them off to the landfill. These clippings quickly decompose, returning essential nutrients to the soil and promoting a healthier lawn.

The history of grasscycling goes back to the very origins of lawn care. In fact, before the invention of lawnmowers with grass catchers, all grass was effectively grasscycled. Only with the introduction of bagging mowers the idea of collecting and discarding grass clippings took root. This became so widespread that many people saw it as the standard way of doing things.

However, the environmental movement of the late 20th century prompted a reevaluation of many traditional practices, including lawn care. The huge volumes of yard waste ending up in landfills (which occupied valuable space and generated greenhouse gases) were recognized as a significant issue.

This awareness led to the resurgence of grasscycling. The benefits of this practice, such as reducing waste and nourishing the soil, aligned perfectly with the growing interest in sustainable living. Today, grasscycling is widely recommended by environmental organizations, agricultural extension services, and many lawn care professionals.

To illustrate, imagine mowing your lawn on a sunny Saturday. Instead of following the usual routine of gathering up the clippings and filling up bag after bag, you simply leave them where they fall. It may seem strange at first. Yet, within a few days, those clippings disappear, decomposing and blending into the lawn. You've just grasscycled, turning your mowing chore into an act of eco-friendly lawn care.

In the following pages, we'll delve deeper into the science behind grasscycling, its multiple benefits, and how to implement it effectively in your lawn care routine.

How to Start Grasscycling

Let's begin with the equipment. While specialized mulching mowers are available, grasscycling doesn't necessarily require you to invest in new machinery. Any lawn mower can grasscycle. Mulching mowers, or mowers with a mulching feature, cut grass blades into smaller pieces that decompose more rapidly. However, if you already have a standard mower, don't fret. It can still do the job, though the clippings may be a bit larger and take a tad longer to decompose. The key is to ensure your mower blades are sharp. Sharp blades make clean cuts, while dull blades tear the grass, leading to a ragged edge that can turn brown. Regularly sharpening your mower blades can result in a healthier-looking lawn.

Now, let's discuss mowing techniques. While it might seem like mowing is a straightforward task, a few strategies can make your grasscycling experience more effective. First, remember the "one-third rule." It's best never to cut more than one-third of the grass blade at a time. This approach results in smaller clippings that decompose more quickly and reduces stress on the grass, promoting healthier growth. For example, if your grass type is healthiest at three inches, aim to mow before it exceeds 4.5 inches. This way, you only remove a third of the grass blade length.

Another helpful strategy is to mow when the grass is dry. Mowing wet grass can lead to clumping of grass clippings, which can smother and discolor the lawn. Dry clippings spread more evenly and decompose faster. Plus, mowing when the lawn is dry is safer to prevent slips and the mower from clogging.

Finally, alternate your mowing pattern. If you mow in the same direction every time, your grass will begin to lean and grow in that direction. By varying your pattern, you'll encourage the grass to grow straighter and healthier. You might mow north to south during one session, then east to west the next.

Timing your mowing is also crucial. Mowing frequency should be based on the growth rate of your grass, not the day of the week. In the fast-growing spring season, you may need to mow more often to maintain the one-third rule. Conversely, the mowing frequency may decrease in the slower growing periods or drought conditions of summer.

Starting grasscycling is that simple. With your existing equipment, by following these mowing techniques and timing tips, you can quickly begin reaping the benefits of this eco-friendly practice.

Managing Potential Issues

If you are a novice in composting activities, you may come across some potential problems or concerns. Fear not! These are typical and can be easily managed with the correct information and strategies. Let's address some of these:

1. Concerns About Thatch

Thatch is a layer of mainly dead grass tissue that can build up between healthy green grass and the soil. Some people fear that grasscycling contributes to thatch build-up. Thatch chiefly comprises tougher plant parts like stems and roots that decompose slowly. Grass clippings, on the other hand, are mostly water and decompose rapidly, returning valuable nutrients to the soil rather than contributing to the thatch layer.

If you notice an excessive thatch build-up in your lawn, it's more likely due to over-watering, over-fertilizing, or mowing too infrequently rather than grasscycling. If thatch becomes a problem, consider aeration techniques or dethatching tools to manage it.

2. Dealing with Long Grass Clippings

Long grass clippings can be a bit more challenging because they may not decompose as rapidly and can form unsightly clumps. To prevent this, adhere to the one-third rule discussed earlier: only mow one-third of the grass blade's length at a time. If circumstances prevent this and you end up with long clippings, consider going over them a second time with the mower to chop them up into smaller pieces that will decompose faster and be less likely to form clumps.

3. Grasscycling with Pets

Pets, especially dogs, love to roll in and play on the lawn. Grasscycling doesn't interfere with this, but there are some things to remember. First, ensure the grass clippings are free from harmful pesticides or other chemicals that could affect your pet's health. Second, while grass clippings aren't harmful to dogs, some might get too curious and try eating them. If your dog tends to do this, keep an eye on them while the clippings are fresh. Once the clippings have dried and started decomposing, they are less likely to attract your pet's attention.

Combining Grasscycling with Other Composting Techniques

Grasscycling is a brilliant and effective standalone technique for enriching your lawn. However, the beauty of sustainable practices such as this is that they often complement one another. Combining grasscycling with traditional composting and vermicomposting can allow you to take your green waste management and soil enrichment to the next level.

Using Grass Clippings in Traditional Composting

Grass clippings are a fantastic addition to a traditional compost pile. In composting parlance, they are considered a 'green' material, which means they are high in nitrogen. Greens help to speed up the composting process and provide essential nutrients. They counterbalance 'brown' materials, such as dried leaves or cardboard, which are carbon-rich and give structure to the compost pile.

If you have more grass clippings than your lawn can handle or want to create compost for use in other parts of your garden, you can add grass clippings to your compost pile. Remember, balance is crucial in composting, so you'll want to mix your grass clippings with appropriate browns.

Here's a simple way: Start with a layer of browns at the bottom of your compost pile or bin. Then add a layer of grass clippings. Follow this with another layer of browns. Keep adding layers until the bin is full or you run out of materials. Turning or mixing the compost pile every few weeks will help speed up the decomposition process.

Grasscycling and Vermicomposting

Vermicomposting is another composting technique involving worms (usually red wigglers) to consume organic waste and transform it into nutrient-rich worm castings, a prized soil amendment. Worms love many of the same kitchen scraps that go into traditional compost, but they're also quite fond of grass clippings.

If you've started a worm bin, you can add grass clippings as part of the worms' diet. But, there are a few things to keep in mind. First, as with traditional composting, balance is essential. Worms need a varied diet, so ensure grass clippings are only a part of what you feed them.

Second, grass clippings can heat up as they decompose, potentially harming your worms if they make up a large portion of the bin content. To avoid this, add grass clippings in moderation and mix them with other worm-friendly foods. Also, ensure the clippings are pesticide-free, as worms are sensitive to chemicals.

Sheet Composting: The Art of Lasagna Gardening

O ften called "lasagna gardening," this method presents a fresh approach to composting that's practical, versatile, and delightfully easy. Perfect for beginners, sheet composting takes its cue from the tasty Italian dish it's named after, building layer upon layer of organic materials to create a hearty, nutrient-dense feast for your garden.

The essence of sheet composting lies in its simplicity. Instead of maintaining a traditional compost pile, organic materials are directly layered onto the garden bed, where they gradually decompose to improve the health of the soil underneath. The "lasagna" comparison becomes apparent as green and brown organic materials are stacked in layers, much like the pasta, cheese, and sauce in a lasagna dish

But why use this method, you might wonder? Much like preparing a lasagna is a creative way to combine various ingredients into a tasty meal, sheet composting is an innovative and straightforward way to combine different types of organic materials, each providing its unique benefits, into a rich, fertile garden bed.

Interestingly, sheet composting is not a novel concept. Its origins can be traced back to nature itself. If you think about it, Mother Nature has been doing her version of sheet composting for millions of years. Each year, leaves fall onto the forest floor and other plant and animal waste, creating layers of organic material that decompose over time, enriching the soil and promoting the growth of new life. Inspired by this natural process, gardeners have simply taken it and given it a name and a method.

The term "lasagna gardening" was popularized by Patricia Lanza in her 1998 book "Lasagna Gardening: A New Layering System for Bountiful Gardens." In her book,

Lanza describes a garden bed preparation method involving layering organic materials, with no need for tilling or removing existing sod or weeds. The method was named "lasagna gardening" for its similarity to making lasagna - layering different ingredients to create something extraordinary.

Building Your Organic Lasagna

Just like the famous Italian dish, the "lasagna" in your garden will require a variety of ingredients. These will come in the form of organic waste, specifically categorized into two color-coded groups: green and brown. If you remember from our previous discussions, these colors don't necessarily refer to the actual hues of the materials but symbolize their roles and nutrient contents in the composting process.

The Green Layer

Green materials are rich in nitrogen, which is crucial for the growth and development of microorganisms that facilitate the composting process. Think of them as the protein in your lasagna, fueling the microorganisms' activity. These green ingredients include:

- Kitchen scraps: fruit and vegetable peels, coffee grounds, and tea bags are excellent green materials. But remember, no processed foods, oils, or animal products besides eggshells!

- Fresh green yard waste: grass clippings, fresh leaves, and plant trimmings serve as a superb source of nitrogen.

- Manure: If you have access to it, herbivore manure (like from cows, horses, or chickens) can be an excellent green addition.

The Brown Layer

Contrasting the green materials, brown materials are rich in carbon, providing energy and structure to your compost. They are the pasta sheets of your garden lasagna, offering form and sustenance to the compost pile. Typical brown materials include:

- Dry yard waste: Dried leaves, straw, and small twigs are typical brown materials.

- Non-glossy paper materials: Newspaper, plain cardboard, and non-glossy junk mail can also be included. Just be sure they're shredded or torn into smaller pieces to aid in their decomposition.

- Wood chips or sawdust: These can be excellent brown materials, but use them sparingly, as they can take longer to break down.

Now, the magic of sheet composting happens when these green and brown layers alternate, starting and ending with a brown layer. This structure ensures an ideal environment for decomposition, providing a balanced diet for the microorganisms at work.

Optional Boosters

In addition to green and brown materials, some optional "boosters" can kickstart your composting process or add extra nutrients to your compost. These might be the cheese or seasoning in your lasagna, enhancing the overall result. They include:

- Compost activator: This product, available at garden stores, contains microorganisms to jump-start the composting process. It's not necessary, but it can speed things up if you're in a hurry.

- Garden soil or finished compost: Adding a thin layer of garden soil or finished compost can introduce beneficial microorganisms to your pile.

- Eggshells: Crushed eggshells add calcium to your compost, an essential nutrient for plant health.

Step-by-Step Guide to Sheet Composting

The journey to a thriving lasagna garden starts with choosing the right spot, gathering your materials, and understanding how to assemble and maintain your compost pile effectively. In this section, we'll take you step-by-step through this process, turning what might seem daunting into an exciting and rewarding gardening experience.

Choosing the Right Location

Practicing sheet composting is like preparing to cook a hearty lasagna in your kitchen. Before you even preheat your oven or gather your ingredients, you need to make sure you've got the right kitchen layout, haven't you? Similarly, setting up your lasagna garden, or a sheet composting bed, begins with selecting the perfect spot. This choice is a crucial first step and requires a discerning eye and a bit of strategic thinking.

Imagine, if you will, the golden rays of the sun. Your plants, like sunbathers, are yearning for it. They crave it for their growth, for the process known as photosynthesis. Picture a place in your yard where sunlight dances freely for about six to eight hours a day. That sunny stage is the ideal arena for your lasagna garden. Just the right balance of sunlight can work wonders for your sheet composting journey and, ultimately, your garden's vitality.

Now, let's talk about water. Just as we humans need water to survive and thrive, your lasagna garden thirsts for moisture. The decomposition process, the crux of composting, is a bit like a backstage crew working tirelessly behind the scenes to break down organic matter. But they need the right conditions to carry out their duties, and moisture is a significant part of this equation. Therefore, it's wise to choose a location within arm's reach of a water source. This will make the job of hydrating your compost pile a breeze rather than a chore.

Lastly, let's consider space - the canvas upon which you'll paint your lasagna garden masterpiece. The size of your canvas will be dictated by the volume of compostable materials at your disposal and the space available within your yard. A standard lasagna bed, a modest tower of alternating organic layers, stands about two feet tall. However, the beauty of this composting method is its flexibility. Your lasagna garden can be as petite or grand as suits your needs and available resources.

Layering Your Materials

With the location chosen and the materials collected, it's time to build your lasagna. Follow these steps to layer your materials effectively:

1. Start with a Brown Layer: Your first layer should be a thick layer of brown materials. This could be a layer of cardboard or several layers of newspaper, which will smother any existing grass or weeds. Wet this layer to start the decomposition process.

2. Add a Green Layer: The second layer should be your nitrogen-rich green materials. Think of your kitchen scraps, fresh grass clippings, or manure. This layer can be around 2-4 inches thick.

3. Alternate Layers: Now, repeat the process, adding a brown layer followed by a green one. Aim to make your brown layers about twice as thick as your green layers, but don't worry if the ratios aren't perfect.

4. End with a Brown Layer: Your last layer should be brown materials to help deter pests. If you don't have enough brown materials, don't worry. You can always add more as you collect them.

Maintaining and Watering Your Lasagna Garden

Unlike traditional composting methods, a lasagna garden requires very little maintenance. Here are some tips to ensure your lasagna garden thrives:

• Keep it Moist: Moisture is crucial for decomposition. The compost pile should be as damp as a wrung-out sponge. Water it regularly to maintain the right moisture level.

• Add Layers as Needed: As you produce more kitchen scraps or yard waste, you can add them to your lasagna garden. Just remember to always try to cover green materials with brown materials.

• Patience is Key: Remember, decomposition takes time. Your lasagna garden might take several months to decompose enough for planting. The good news is, you can start a lasagna garden any time of year. If you start in the fall, it will be ready for planting in the spring.

The Sheet Composting Timeline

Understanding the timeframe for sheet composting—how long it takes and how to recognize when it's ready—can be like deciphering a natural mystery or even reading an exciting book. The chapters unfold slowly, revealing more depth and complexity as you delve deeper. But fear not! With some guidance and patience, you'll become proficient at decoding this narrative and timing your composting efforts just right.

Let's start with the basic question: How long does a sheet compost or lasagna garden take to decompose? The answer is not straightforward because it relies on several factors, much like cooking times vary depending on the ingredients and cooking methods used. The decomposition process depends on the types of materials used, their sizes, the environmental conditions, and even the local microorganism population. But to give you a rough estimate, most lasagna gardens are ready for planting after about six months to a year. Starting your compost pile in the fall gives it the entire winter to break down, and by spring, your garden bed should be primed for planting.

But how do you know when your lasagna garden is ready? There are some telltale signs that your sheet compost has fully decomposed and is ready to nourish your plants. Here's what to look out for:

1. No Recognizable Layers: In a fully composted lasagna garden, the original layers of green and brown materials will no longer be distinct. They will have combined into a rich, dark, crumbly material that resembles high-quality garden soil.

2. Unidentified Compostable Items: While some resistant materials like twigs or eggshells might still be identifiable, most compost material should be indistinguishable from the rest.

3. Earthly Aroma: Your compost pile should have a pleasant, earthy smell, much like a forest after a rainstorm. Detecting any foul or off-putting odors may indicate that the composting process is incomplete or that there is an imbalance in your compost pile.

4. Warm, but not Hot: A composting pile generates heat as a byproduct of the decomposition process. However, once the composting process is complete, the pile should feel warm or have returned to the ambient temperature, but it should not feel hot to the touch.

Common Mistakes and Effective Solutions

Starting a new adventure, whether it's sheet composting or a hiking trip, often comes with a few missteps. But these stumbling blocks, rather than hindrances, can become stepping stones to learning, refining, and mastering your composting skills. Here, we'll explore some common mistakes new composters often make and offer advice on how to navigate them with confidence. We've transformed potential pitfalls into learning opportunities, all with the goal of bolstering your journey toward successful sheet composting.

Layer Imbalance: One frequent mistake beginners often make is creating uneven layers of green (nitrogen-rich) and brown (carbon-rich) materials. This imbalance can slow the decomposition process and produce a less nutritious compost. The trick to sidestep this pitfall is to understand the 'lasagna' analogy fully. Much like you wouldn't pile too much cheese or tomato sauce in one layer of your lasagna, aim for a balanced layering of green and brown materials in your compost. A typical ratio is 2:1 of browns to greens.

- Lack of Moisture: Sheet composting, like all forms of composting, requires a Goldilocks balance of moisture. Too little, and the decomposition process slows down; too much, and you might create an environment conducive to unwanted pests and odors. Think of your compost pile as a sponge; it should be damp but not soaking. If your compost pile looks dry, don't hesitate to sprinkle some water to bring it back to the optimal moisture level.

- Insufficient Material Size: The larger the pieces of material you add to your compost, the longer it will take to decompose. A garden filled with large branches and whole vegetable scraps will take much longer to become compost than one filled with small twigs and chopped-up kitchen waste. Therefore, breaking your compost materials into smaller pieces can speed up the decomposition process and yield quicker results.

- Neglecting the Compost: Sheet composting is a relatively low-maintenance composting method, but it doesn't mean you can set it and forget it entirely. Regular checks for moisture balance, temperature, and general progress can ensure your compost stays on track. This simple act of attention can mean the difference between a thriving compost pile and one that's struggling.

- Impatience: Lastly, one common mistake that isn't related to the physical compost pile but rather the composter: impatience. Remember, decomposition is a natural process, and it takes time. Don't rush it. If you're new to composting, it can be easy to get anxious about why your compost isn't 'ready' yet. But patience, in composting as in life, often yields the best results.

Consider these common pitfalls as companions on your composting journey, reminding you to balance, observe, moderate, and be patient.

BOOK IV

URBAN & INDOOR COMPOSTING

SUSTAINABLE WASTE SOLUTIONS
FOR CITY DWELLERS

As we navigate the densely populated cityscapes of the 21st century, the need for sustainable, space-efficient practices have never been more pronounced.

This book provides a comprehensive guide for urban residents, revealing how they can convert their kitchen scraps and other organic waste into nutrient-rich compost, even within limited living spaces. We will explore innovative methods tailored for urban and indoor settings, and how these contribute to a sustainable lifestyle, helping city dwellers play their part in waste reduction and ecological preservation.

Whether you reside in an apartment, a townhouse, or a single-family home in the city, this chapter will equip you with the tools and knowledge to start composting right where you are.

Composting in Urban Settings: Overcoming Space Constraints

Imagine turning your kitchen scraps into nutrient-rich soil, even in the throbbing heart of a metropolis. This eco-friendly practice allows city dwellers to contribute to the health of our planet without requiring vast outdoor spaces or rural backyards. Sounds terrific, doesn't it?

Urban composting, simply put, is the process of composting organic waste within city confines. It's a tailor-made solution for those living in apartments, condominiums, or houses with small yards. Despite the hustle and constant hum of city life around you, you can participate in this green initiative right in your kitchen or balcony.

But why should you consider composting in an urban setting? It's a simple act that fosters sustainability, reduces your carbon footprint, and brings you closer to nature, even within the steel and glass landscape of the city. The importance and benefits are manifold. Not only does it reduce the amount of waste sent to landfills, but it also enriches the soil of your potted plants or community gardens.

So, are you ready to embrace urban composting and transform your waste into wealth? Let's explore how to overcome the challenges and make the most out of your limited space.

Challenges in Urban Composting

Urban composting comes with challenges that we need to address before successfully setting up a system. Here are the primary hurdles that you may encounter:

- Space Constraints: In high-density urban settings, every square foot counts. Many city dwellers live in apartments with no outdoor spaces, and if there is an outdoor area, it's typically a small balcony or shared yard. Traditional compost piles or bins can be quite large and may not fit in such limited spaces.

- Odor Control: Living close to neighbors means you have to be extra considerate. If not properly managed, odors from a compost pile can become a nuisance, potentially leading to conflicts.

- Pest Management: Pests can pose a significant problem in communal living spaces. If not well-maintained, your compost pile can attract unwanted visitors like rodents or insects, creating another set of issues.

- Lack of Green Waste: Unlike rural or suburban homes with gardens, urban homes may not have easy access to green waste like grass clippings or fallen leaves, which are essential components for a healthy compost pile.

Types of Composting Suitable for Urban Areas

Ah, the urban composter: a modern-day superhero thriving in the heart of concrete jungles, turning waste into treasure. Just as every superhero has a superpower, so too does the urban composter have their unique abilities. Theirs is not the strength of ten men or the ability to fly, but rather, it is the power of versatility.

Take, for instance, the magic of worm composting. This process, also known as vermicomposting, transforms the urban composter into a veritable worm whisperer. They employ a legion of wriggly allies, turning a heap of organic waste into nutrient-rich compost. Right there, under the kitchen sink or on a secluded balcony corner, a silent, efficient, and completely odorless process unfolds. As the worms work their magic, the composter's everyday scraps become a gardener's gold.

Then there's the art of Bokashi composting, a skill that borrows from the age-old tradition of fermentation. With this method, the urban composter morphs into a culinary alchemist. Instead of transforming grapes into wine or cabbage into sauerkraut, they're fermenting kitchen scraps. A special bran teeming with beneficial microbes aids in this process, ensuring the composting is swift and surprisingly smell-free. And the stage for this marvel of waste alchemy? It could be as simple as a small bucket tucked away in a kitchen corner or a quiet spot on the balcony.

Indoor composting is yet another feather in the urban composter's cap. Various indoor composting methods and tools, from state-of-the-art to chic designer models or simple homemade variants, come into play here. These systems are tailored to fit snugly into the smallest spaces while ensuring an odor-free environment. With this method, you become a master of space, making composting possible even in the most cramped apartments.

Urban Composting Solutions

Urban composting often demands more creativity and resourcefulness than composting in rural or suburban settings. Thankfully, a variety of clever solutions have been designed to cater to the unique circumstances of city life. Here are some popular composting systems specifically designed for urban environments.

- Compost Tumblers: Compost tumblers are a fantastic option for urban composting, providing a neat, contained, and efficient way to compost your organic waste. These closed systems are typically mounted on a stand and can be spun to mix the composting materials, thus eliminating the need for manual turning. They're compact, keep pests out, and speed up the composting process by promoting aeration.

- Stackable Compost Bins: Stackable compost bins are another excellent option for small spaces. These systems typically involve a series of trays stacked one on top of another. Fresh waste is added to the top tray, and as it breaks down, it moves through the trays until it becomes finished compost at the bottom. This vertical design is a space saver, making the composting process quite easy.

- Indoor Compost Bins: For those without any outdoor space, indoor compost bins can be a lifesaver. These bins are designed to be small enough to fit under a kitchen sink or in a closet, and most importantly, they are constructed to prevent any foul smells from escaping. They can be paired with a Bokashi system or a worm bin to effectively compost kitchen scraps right in your home.

- Community Composting Initiatives: If personal composting seems too daunting or space is too tight, community composting initiatives can be a great solution. These programs often involve a community garden or a local organization where residents can drop off their compostable materials. Not only does this solution divert waste from the landfill, but it also fosters a sense of community and shared environmental responsibility.

Maximizing Small Spaces for Composting

Every inch of space is valuable in the compact world of the urban composter. It's like a game of Tetris; only instead of fitting digital shapes together, we're trying to squeeze every last bit of composting potential out of our living spaces. So, how do we win this game? Here are some strategies:

Firstly, let's think vertically. Just as skyscrapers allow us to make the most out of a small footprint, vertical composting lets us take full advantage of the height available. Consider using stackable compost bins or worm towers that ascend upwards rather than sprawling outwards. This way, your composting operation can stretch toward the sky, leaving your precious floor space free for other uses.

Have you ever considered the potential of your balcony? This often-overlooked space can be a gold mine for composting. A small compost tumbler or a Bokashi bucket can easily fit into a corner without dominating the space. If you're worried about aesthetics, there are plenty of stylish composting solutions that will blend seamlessly with your outdoor decor. Your balcony is not just for sipping coffee or growing plants; it's also a platform for your waste transformation mission!

Unleash your creativity and embrace flexibility to take your composting efforts to new exciting levels. Your composting system should adapt to your space, not the other way around. If a traditional compost pile doesn't fit, maybe a worm bin under the kitchen sink will. If your balcony is too sunny for composting, perhaps a shaded corner in your living room can host a Bokashi bucket.

Community Composting: Turning Constraints into Opportunity

In the midst of urban life, with its towering buildings and ceaseless activity, the practice of composting can seem like a distant reality. Yet, it is within these concrete jungles that community composting programs have begun to flourish.

Community composting is an outstanding example of the community spirit inherent in city living. This shared endeavor transforms what might seem like a solitary act into a communal effort, providing a viable and impactful solution for composting in areas with limited individual space.

Here are some key benefits of community composting:

- Waste Reduction: Community composting significantly decreases the amount of organic waste that ends up in landfills. This helps reduce methane emissions, a potent greenhouse gas contributing to climate change.

- Environmental Education: Participating in a community composting program can be an educational experience. It offers a hands-on way to learn about the composting process and the broader concepts of waste management and sustainability.

- Community Building: Community composting fosters a sense of unity and shared purpose among participants. It can strengthen community ties and promote cooperation.

- Improved Soil Health: The finished compost produced can be used to enhance the soil in community gardens and green spaces. This leads to healthier plants and a more vibrant local environment.

- Resource Efficiency: By pooling resources, community composting programs can often afford to invest in larger, more efficient composting systems. This can lead to faster composting times and higher-quality compost.

- Accessibility: Community composting can make the benefits of composting accessible to individuals who may not have the space or resources to compost on their own.

Community composting programs can take many forms. They can be as simple as a shared compost bin in a community garden or as organized as city-wide composting initiatives with designated collection points. The versatility of these programs makes them adaptable to various urban settings, from high-rise apartment blocks to sprawling residential neighborhoods.

Success Stories of Urban Composting

Urban composting is not just a concept; it's a reality that's thriving in many corners of the world. The success stories of communities who have embraced the practice are both motivational and educational, showcasing the potential of urban composting in the real world.

San Francisco

Back in 1996, San Francisco was the first city in the US to start a big program for composting food waste. The city reached a goal of keeping 50 percent of its waste out of landfills in 2000. In 2002, they decided to try for even more. They set a new goal of keeping 75 percent of waste out of landfills by 2010 and aimed for zero waste by 2020. In 2009, the city ruled that everyone living or working in San Francisco had to recycle and compost.

In 2012, the city of San Francisco achieved something impressive. They managed to keep more than 80 percent of all their waste out of landfills. This means they found other ways to use or eliminate garbage, a big part of their famous zero-waste program. This program is admired around the world. San Francisco did this through several methods. They made rules about waste, gave people incentives to reduce waste, provided three different bins for different kinds of waste, and educated the people living and working in the city about waste in many other languages.

Buffalo

Farmer Pirates Compost, a Buffalo-based composting initiative, was informally established in 2012 by a cohort of urban farmers needing high-quality compost. Officially providing composting services and compost to the Buffalo region since 2014, the organization strives to facilitate easy and cost-effective composting for households and businesses. Their mission involves surmounting the challenges of urban agriculture by pooling resources, including knowledge, land, equipment, and supplies.

The group primarily farms on vacant residential land, necessitating substantial soil improvement. Compost is vital in this process, contributing to sustainable, healthy food production. Despite relying on aged horse bedding from outside the city, Farmer Pirates aims to increase their capacity to manage compost made from food waste, which is plentiful in the city and boasts richer fertility.

Originating from a Kickstarter campaign, the organization has evolved into a well-honed service with roughly 400 residential members and several larger commercial composters, fostering optimism for the future of composting in Buffalo.

UC San Diego

Mesa Nueva Community: A group of students established a composting system in the Mesa Nueva community garden in October 2022. The system includes three compost bins: one open for adding compost and two closed for composting. The waste decomposition process usually takes around two to four weeks to be made into compost. The compost bins are centrally located, making it easy for residents to drop off compostable waste. The compost team notifies gardeners when the fresh dirt is available after sifting, so they can bring the compost back into the community to use for gardening.

While the project has faced staffing challenges, it has successfully reduced methane emissions and the climate footprint of the community. The students are working to create a part-time paid position to ensure the project's long-term sustainability.

Indoor Composting Techniques: Solutions for Small Spaces

Indoor composting is a reality for many urban dwellers who have embraced this eco-friendly practice. As our urban landscapes continue to expand, so does the need for sustainable, creative solutions to waste management - and this is where indoor composting shines.

So, what exactly is indoor composting? Simply put, it's the process of recycling your organic waste - think vegetable peels, coffee grounds, or dead houseplant leaves - inside your home rather than in an outdoor compost pile or bin. This process transforms your kitchen scraps into a nutrient-rich soil amendment, perfect for your indoor plants or balcony garden.

While the idea of composting indoors might initially raise eyebrows, it's a trend that's gaining momentum, particularly in homes that lack outdoor space. Apartment dwellers, in particular, are finding value in this practice as it offers a practical and effective way to reduce waste and contribute to a healthier environment, all from the comfort of their own home. The beauty of indoor composting is that it offers a possible path to sustainability, regardless of where you live or how much outdoor space you have at your disposal.

Types of Indoor Composting

Navigating the world of indoor composting can be like stepping into a bustling farmer's market - there's a lot to choose from, and each method has its unique charm. Here are a few popular indoor composting techniques:

- Vermicomposting: This method relies on our wriggly friends - the worms. Specifically, red wigglers are often used. These worms consume organic waste, and their castings (worm poop, essentially) is a nutrient-rich compost. You only need a worm bin, bedding material, and kitchen scraps.

- Electric Composting: Electric composting could be the answer for those who prefer a more high-tech approach. These devices accelerate the composting process using heat and aeration. They are compact, odorless, and can turn your kitchen waste into compost in a matter of hours.

- Bokashi Composting: This Japanese method involves fermenting your kitchen waste in a sealed bin with special bran infused with beneficial microbes. It's an odorless process that can handle almost all types of kitchen waste, including things like meat and dairy that aren't typically compostable.

In addition to these methods, indoor composting bins or tumblers can also be used. These containers are designed to facilitate composting while being small enough to fit comfortably inside your home. Each method has its pros and cons, so it's all about finding the one that best fits your lifestyle and composting goals.

Setting Up an Indoor Compost System

Let's map out the steps to establishing your indoor composting system:

1. Choosing the Right System: Depending on your composting method, you'll need to get your hands on the right gear. It could be a worm bin for vermicomposting, an electric composter, or a Bokashi bin. Each has its requirements, so you'll need to do some homework to determine which suits you best.

2. Selecting the Ideal Location: The location of your compost bin can make a significant difference in your composting journey. Ideally, it should be in a spot that's easily accessible yet out of the way. It could be a corner of your kitchen, a utility room, or a balcony. Remember, if you're choosing vermicomposting, the worms need a dark and cool place.

3. Knowing What to Compost: Indoor composting can handle a variety of kitchen waste, but there are still a few things to keep in mind. While methods like Bokashi can handle almost anything, traditional composting, and vermicomposting have a few restrictions. Meat, dairy, and oily foods are typically a no-go.

4. Managing Odor and Pests: One of the main concerns with indoor composting is managing odor and pests. This is where a well-maintained compost system shines. If the balance of greens and browns is right and the compost is turned regularly, it should not emit unpleasant odors. As for pests, keeping the compost bin properly sealed should keep them at bay.

Maintaining Your Indoor Compost

When we initiate the process of indoor composting, nurturing our tiny indoor compost system becomes as crucial as caring for a garden. It's here where we don our maintenance hats, tending to our compost as we would our cherished plants.

As mentioned earlier, maintaining balance is fundamental for our indoor compost setup. We need to add an even mix of green materials, such as vegetable scraps that are rich in nitrogen, and brown materials, like shredded paper or dry leaves that are high in carbon. The recommended ratio is two parts brown materials to one part green materials. However, slight variations in this ratio are fine and won't cause any significant issues.

Just as we enjoy a breath of fresh air every now and then, so too does our compost. Oxygen invigorates the composting process, and we introduce it by aerating or turning the compost. It's a refreshing stir in the life of our compost, the frequency of which depends on the composting method we've chosen.

As with baking a loaf of bread or a batch of cookies, recognizing the signs is the key to realizing when our compost is ready. Finished compost greets us with a pleasant, earthy smell and crumbly texture reminiscent of fertile garden soil. It's a sight for sore eyes, rich and dark brown in color. If we spot any identifiable food scraps, we simply give it more time.

Patience takes center stage in the play of composting. It's a natural process that unfolds in its own time. As we sit back and let nature perform, we find ourselves rewarded with 'black gold,' a tangible symbol of our progress in composting and a true blessing for our plants.

Using Your Indoor Compost

As the wheel of composting turns full circle, it's time to introduce the fruits of your labor - the nutrient-rich compost - to your indoor green companions. This black gold can give a new life to your houseplants, making them thrive and shine with vitality. It can also turn your balcony or window box planters into fertile oases brimming with healthy, happy plants.

But the scope of your indoor compost doesn't have to be limited to your home. If you have surplus compost, consider sharing this wealth with your local community garden. This way, you're not only contributing to the health of a broader range of plants but also fostering a sense of community around sustainable practices.

The act of using your compost brings closure to the composting cycle, but it also marks the start of a new journey. As your plants grow, they will create more organic waste, which can, in turn, be composted. It's a beautiful, self-sustaining cycle that nurtures both the earth and our connection to it.

Benefits and Challenges of Indoor Composting

Like any practice, indoor composting has its benefits and challenges. However, with a bit of creativity and determination, these challenges can be transformed into opportunities for growth and learning.

Benefits:

1. Accessibility: Regardless of living situation, anyone can compost indoors.

2. Waste Reduction: It allows us to reduce our environmental impact by recycling organic waste.

3. Nutrient-Rich Compost: It provides homemade compost for indoor plants, balcony gardens, or local community gardens.

Challenges and Solutions:

1. Odor Management: A bad smell can indicate an imbalance in the compost. This can usually be fixed by adding more brown materials or ensuring the compost is well-aerated.

2. Pest Control: Most indoor composting systems are designed to keep pests

out. If pests appear, adding a layer of brown material on top of the compost can be effective.

3. Space Constraints: There are many compact composting systems available that can fit even the smallest spaces. Choosing the right strategy can make composting possible, regardless of your living space size.

Environmental Impact and Resource Conservation

Composting is an age-old practice, but it's never been more relevant than in today's urban and indoor spaces. Urban and indoor composting brings the cycle of life right to your doorstep. It allows you to witness directly how nature cleverly recycles its resources, transforming what seems to be waste into a nutrient-rich medium for new growth. It's about participating directly in this cycle, understanding the interconnectedness of life, and making a real, tangible contribution to the health of our planet.

Environmental Impact

The environmental impact of urban and indoor composting is profound. These methods solve the practical problem of waste management in limited spaces and contribute significantly to creating a more sustainable and healthier planet. When we compost in our urban apartments or indoor spaces, we play an active role in mitigating some of the pressing environmental issues of our time.

Here are the most significant environmental benefits of urban and indoor composting:

- Waste Reduction: Every year, tons of waste are generated worldwide, much of which ends up in landfills. This overwhelming amount of waste contributes to environmental pollution and the depletion of natural resources. Urban and indoor composting offer a solution by turning organic waste into valuable compost, like food scraps and yard waste. This process significantly reduces the volume of waste each household produces, lightening the load on our landfills. The more we compost, the less waste we generate.

- Lowering Greenhouse Gas Emissions: The decomposition of organic waste in landfills occurs in an oxygen-deprived environment, leading to the production of methane, a potent greenhouse gas that contributes to climate change. However, composting is an aerobic process, meaning it happens in the presence of oxygen. This difference in the decomposition process means that composting produces significantly less methane than landfill decomposition, thus helping to minimize our greenhouse gas emissions.

- Soil Health: Compost is often called 'black gold' for the soil. It is rich in nutrients and beneficial microorganisms that improve soil health. Adding compost to the soil increases its fertility and stimulates healthy root development in plants. Moreover, it improves the soil structure and increases its capacity to retain water and nutrients. All these factors contribute to a robust soil ecosystem, which results in healthier and more resilient plants.

- Water Conservation: Water scarcity is a major concern in many parts of the world. Water conservation is another area where composting might help. Healthy soil with a good structure and high organic matter content can hold more water. Adding compost to the soil increases its water-holding capacity, reducing the need for frequent watering and conserving water.

- Erosion Control: Soil erosion is a significant issue, especially in urban areas where concrete structures have replaced natural landscapes. Erosion removes the topmost, nutrient-rich layer of soil, degrading land quality and leading to landslides and water pollution. Compost can help control erosion. By improving soil structure, compost increases the soil's capacity to absorb and hold water, reducing runoff during heavy rains.

Resource Conservation

Resource conservation is an important cornerstone of sustainability, and composting is pivotal in this endeavor. When we compost, we're not just reducing the amount of waste we send to landfills; we're actually giving back to the earth, creating a beautiful cycle of growth, consumption, decay, and rebirth.

Composting, especially in the heart of the concrete jungle, can feel like a small revolution against the industrialized food chain. Whenever we toss our kitchen scraps into the compost bin instead of the trash, we're stepping away from reliance on synthetic fertilizers. While these chemical concoctions might boost plant growth in the short term, they often leave our soils depleted and lifeless in the long run. Compost, on the other hand, contains an abundance of life and nutrients, naturally and sustainably enriching our soils.

Moreover, compost has an incredible ability to hold onto water. Very little of it gets a chance to soak into the ground and nourish plant life. This might seem like a minor superpower, but in our urban environments, water often simply runs off the concrete and asphalt, rushing into sewers and waterways. By adding compost to our urban green spaces, we can significantly improve the soil's capacity to retain water, giving our plants a longer drink while conserving this precious resource.

Community and Economic Benefits

Composting, while an environmentally conscious act, also offers a myriad of community and economic benefits that might leave you more stunned.

Firstly, composting can significantly reduce waste disposal costs. Every apple core, coffee ground, or leafy green that you add to your compost pile is one less item taking up space in your trash bag. This might seem trivial on an individual level, but consider the impact if an entire apartment complex, neighborhood, or city took up composting. The reduction in waste volume could potentially save municipalities substantial amounts of money on waste collection and disposal.

Another economic benefit is tied to local food production. As urban composting gains momentum, it provides an opportunity for urban farming to thrive. Compost enriches the soil, making it fertile and ready for planting. This can lead to an increase in local food production, reducing dependence on imported foods. It's a simple equation: less distance traveled equals less carbon emissions and fresher, more nutrient-dense food for urban dwellers. Furthermore, selling locally grown produce can help the local economy and create job opportunities.

Community connections are another often overlooked benefit of urban and indoor composting. Joining a community composting program can be a fantastic way to meet like-minded individuals in your area, fostering a sense of belonging and shared purpose. Composting can bring people together, united by a common goal - to reduce waste and give back to the earth. Schools can introduce composting programs as educational tools, teaching children valuable lessons about nature, responsibility, and the cycle of life.

Health and Well-being

Let's examine how urban and indoor composting can positively influence our health and well-being.

- Sense of Accomplishment: There's something deeply satisfying about turning your kitchen scraps into a valuable resource for your plants. Every time you add compost to your plants and see them thrive, you'll be reminded of your direct contribution to that success.

- Connection with Nature: Composting can help bridge the gap between urban living and the natural world. Composting brings you in touch with the cycle of life and death, decay and renewal - even in the heart of the city.

- Improves Quality of Home-Grown Produce: Composting can significantly improve the health of your plants and, consequently, any fruits, vegetables, or herbs you grow. Compost provides a rich source of nutrients, leading to healthier plants and tastier produce.

- Stress Relief: Taking care of your compost can be meditative, offering an escape from the digital world to the cycles of nature. The simple act of turning the compost, and checking for the proper moisture and temperature levels, can be a welcome respite from your daily stresses.

- Education and Awareness: Composting can be an excellent educational tool if you have children. It's a practical way to teach them about the environment, the importance of recycling, and how nature works in a cyclical manner.

Now, armed with the knowledge of how composting can positively impact your home and the environment, it's time to take action. Starting your urban or indoor composting practice might seem daunting, but remember, every incredible journey begins with a single step. Whether it's a worm bin under your sink, a Bokashi bucket in your pantry, or an indoor composter in your living room, the perfect composting solution for your home is patience. You have the power to make a significant difference in environmental conservation and sustainability, starting right within your own home.

Techniques and Tips for Urban Composting

C omposting can thrive in your urban spaces, and with a bit of creativity and commitment, it can be just as effective as it is in a sprawling country farm.

Start by finding the right system that works for you. Whether it's a worm bin tucked away in your kitchen cabinet, a sleek, odor-controlled composter that doubles as a countertop decoration, or a shared community composting initiative, there's an option for every apartment, every lifestyle, and every green ambition.

One of the best things about urban composting is the sense of camaraderie it can create. It's not just about making compost; it's about making connections and contributing to your local community. Find a composting buddy, either in your building or your neighborhood, and your journey will become more enjoyable, the problems will be easier to solve, and the rewards doubly satisfying.

As an urban composter, you'll become an expert in the art of layering. A layer of browns (like shredded newspaper or dried leaves), followed by a layer of greens (your kitchen scraps), topped with another layer of browns, will help your compost stay healthy, smell-free, and efficient. It's like making an eco-friendly lasagna right in your own home!

And speaking of kitchen scraps, if you want to become a genuinely efficient urban composter, your freezer and blender will become your best friends. Freezing scraps can keep the pests out and speed up the decomposition process, while blending breaks down the material, making it easier for the microorganisms in your compost to do their work.

Composting, at its heart, is a natural process. Watch how nature handles waste and try to mimic that in your urban composting. With patience and dedication, you'll not only have created a sustainable waste cycle in your own home, but you'll also contribute to a greener, healthier urban environment.

Helpful Tips for Urban Composters

Let's explore some helpful tips that will certainly make urban composting smoother:

- Use a Blender: Another way to speed up decomposition is to blend your kitchen scraps before adding them to your compost bin. Doing so breaks the material down, making it easier for the microorganisms to do their job.

- Explore Technology: There are now smart compost bins that control temperature, aeration, and moisture levels automatically, making composting almost effortless.

- Compost in Your Apartment Balcony: If you have a balcony, consider using it for composting. Composting bins or tumblers can easily fit into this space, and the open-air can help to control odors.

- Maximize Space with Vertical Composting: Vertical composting is a smart way to make the most out of limited space. In this method, compostable materials are stacked in a vertical bin, producing a large amount of compost in a small area.

- Learn from Nature: Nature is the best teacher, right? Observing nature's method of composting in forests and parks can offer great insights. The naturally decomposing leaves and organic materials slowly enrich the soil, creating a fertile bed for new growth. In your composting, try to replicate this natural cycle. Incorporate a diverse mix of materials and maintain a balance, just as nature does.

Smart Tips for Indoor Composting

Let's venture into the world of indoor composting techniques that are efficient and house-friendly. These tips help you to turn your kitchen scraps into nutrient-rich compost without leaving the comfort of your home.

One of the most popular techniques is vermicomposting, or worm composting. Using a special breed of worms known as red wigglers, this method is perfect for apartment dwellers. These tiny creatures work their magic in a compact, odorless worm bin, munching through your organic waste and transforming it into high-quality compost. The bin can be placed under the kitchen sink, in a basement, or even in a closet - making it ideal for space-constrained living.

Then there's Bokashi composting, a traditional Japanese method that uses a specific group of microorganisms to ferment kitchen waste. The Bokashi bin is sealed tight and can sit right in your kitchen, making it a perfect match for indoor composting. The process is quick, and in a couple of weeks, you'll have fermented waste that can be buried in soil, either in your houseplants or outdoor garden, where it breaks down further into nutrient-rich compost.

Finally, there are electric composters. These high-tech systems speed up the composting process using heat and aeration, turning your kitchen scraps into compost in as little as a few hours. Electric composters are compact and efficient, but they do require electricity and a bit of an investment.

Here are some clever tips for your indoor composting:

- Create a DIY Compost Bin with a Trash Can: If you're a fan of DIY projects, you can turn a small, lidded trash can into a compost bin. Drill some holes for aeration, add a layer of dirt to the bottom, and voilà! You're ready to start composting. It's cheap, simple, and can be a fun weekend project.

- Use Coffee Filters as Compost Liners: To make the process of transferring compost easier and cleaner, you can line your compost bucket with a compostable coffee filter. It helps soak up the moisture from your compost materials and keep things neat and tidy.

- Freeze Your Kitchen Scraps: If you're worried about fruit flies or odors, try freezing your kitchen scraps in a container or compostable bag. Once it's full, you can add the frozen waste directly to your compost bin. This will also help to break down the material faster once it begins to compost.

- Try a Rotating Compost Bin: A rotating compost bin could be an excellent option for those with more space who want to speed up the composting process. It helps aerate the compost material and accelerates the decomposition process.

- Use a Carbon Filter: If odors are a concern, look for a compost bin with a carbon filter in the lid. This will help neutralize odors and keep your kitchen smelling fresh.

- Compost Pet Waste: If you have a pet rabbit or hamster, their waste and bedding can be composted. Never compost waste from dogs or cats, though, as it can contain harmful pathogens.

- Use a Compost Thermometer: To ensure your compost pile is at the optimal temperature for decomposition, you can use a compost thermometer. This can be particularly useful for methods like hot composting.

- Worm Variety: If you're practicing vermicomposting, make sure to get the right type of worms. Red wigglers are often the best choice for composting. Ordinary earthworms found in the garden aren't suitable for indoor composting.

- DIY Worm Bin Bedding: You can create a comfortable home for your composting worms using shredded newspaper or cardboard. Just dampen it until it's as wet as a wrung-out sponge. It's a great way to recycle, and the worms will appreciate it!

- Compost Aerator: Regularly turning your compost can speed up the process significantly. But turning your compost with a pitchfork isn't practical if you're composting indoors. Instead, consider buying a compost aerator. It's smaller, cleaner, and does an excellent job of aerating compost.

- Compost Tea: If you're composting indoors, you might as well make full use of the process. The liquid that drains from your compost can be used as "compost tea," a nutrient-rich liquid that your houseplants will love.

Remember, indoor composting, like any new venture, may require some trial and error. But with these tips, you'll be well on your way to becoming a pro indoor composter.

BOOK V

REVITALIZE YOUR GARDEN

SOIL SECRETS FOR A HEALTHY AND FLOURISHING OASIS

For every gardener, the real magic starts beneath the surface with rich soil. "Utilizing Compost in Your Garden" digs into this very magic, showcasing compost as the powerhouse behind an impressive garden. We're not just talking about turning waste into worth; we're revealing the close-knit dance between compost and plants that can transform your backyard into a thriving ecosystem.

Get ready to uncover the secrets of compost tea, the nutrient-dense brew that breathes life into your soil, and the savvy method of crop rotation aided by compost to keep your soil fertile. This book breaks down practical, innovative techniques, focusing on the potent connection between compost and gardening. It's a world where soil is your canvas, compost your color, and your garden the ultimate work of art.

Enriching Your Soil with Compost

Think of adding compost to the soil as breathing life into it - it's like giving a nutrient-packed superfood to your garden. When you introduce compost, you're not just loading the soil with a plethora of essential nutrients. You're also transforming the very fabric of the soil, improving its structure and enabling it to retain water more efficiently. These vital factors elevate your garden's productivity, making your plants healthier and your harvest more bountiful.

The Science of Compost and Soil

Compost and soil work in tandem to form the backbone of a healthy garden. This harmony begins when you add compost to your garden soil, setting off a cascade of beneficial effects that echo through your entire garden.

Let's start with the soil structure. Picture a network of tiny particles bound together in a way that leaves room for air and water channels. That's your garden soil. By adding compost, you're introducing organic matter that binds these particles together, creating what soil scientists call 'aggregates.' These aggregates are crucial for maintaining a porous soil structure, enabling roots to penetrate deeply and water to percolate efficiently.

Moreover, compost acts as a reservoir of nutrients. It's chock-full of essential elements like nitrogen, phosphorus, and potassium - the holy trinity of plant nutrition. As compost breaks down, these nutrients are gradually released, providing a slow, steady buffet for your plants to feast upon.

Additionally, compost has an impressive ability to retain moisture thanks to its sponge-like properties. This not only ensures a steady water supply to your plants but also helps conserve water by reducing evaporation and runoff.

We can say that compost is like a personal trainer for your garden soil, enhancing its physical fitness, nutrient content, and water retention capability. And just as a personal trainer helps you achieve your best performance, compost helps your soil perform at its best, fostering a garden brimming with life and productivity.

Choosing the Right Compost for Your Soil

There are several factors to consider to ensure that you choose the best compost for your garden:

1. Understand Your Soil Type: A key factor in successful gardening is understanding the characteristics of your soil. For example, sandy soil tends to dry out quickly and leach nutrients, so it can benefit greatly from compost. Compost enhances the sandy soil's capacity to retain water and vital nutrients, fostering plant health. On the other hand, clay soil, which

can be heavy and poorly drained, can be significantly improved by adding compost. Compost will introduce more porosity to clay soil, improving its drainage and aeration, which is crucial for root development. But let's not forget about loamy soil, a balance between sandy and clay soil, which many gardeners consider ideal. However, even this soil type can be further enhanced by compost, enriching its nutrient content and optimizing its structure.

2. Know Your Plants' Preferences: Different plants have distinct nutrient needs, so it's crucial to understand what each of your plants requires to thrive. Some plants, such as leafy greens and corn, have a high affinity for nitrogen-rich environments. On the contrary, fruiting and flowering plants often need higher phosphorus and potassium levels. Consequently, choosing a compost with the appropriate nutritional composition that caters to your plants' preferences can significantly benefit their growth.

3. Consider Your Soil pH: The pH level of your soil is vital in nutrient availability for plant uptake. Most plants prefer a slightly acidic to neutral pH range (6.0-7.0), and compost can be an excellent tool to adjust the soil pH closer to this optimal range. Whether your soil is overly acidic or alkaline, compost can help to balance it out, providing a more favorable environment for most plants.

4. Look for Well-Composted Material: Quality compost tends to be dark, crumbly, and exude a pleasant, earthy smell. This signals that the organic material has thoroughly decomposed and is ripe with nutrients. Compost that still contains recognizable food scraps or yard waste has not fully decomposed and may introduce unwanted pests or diseases into your garden.

5. Consider Specialty Composts: Various composts are formulated to meet specific gardening needs. Some are designed for seed starting, some for potting plants, while others are geared toward enriching flower beds. These specialty composts have a unique mix of nutrients optimized for their respective applications and can be an excellent choice if they align with

your gardening needs.

6. Watch Out for Contaminants: You must be wary of compost that may contain harmful substances such as pesticides or herbicides. These substances can hamper plant growth and even contaminate your garden ecosystem. If you ever decide to try the ready composts, pick trusted sources or compost certified by a credible authority to guarantee the absence of such contaminants.

7. Organic is Best: Whenever feasible, go for organic compost. Organic compost is made from materials that have not been treated with synthetic chemicals. As a result, it is devoid of any synthetic residues that could harm your plants or the broader environment. You are fostering a healthier, more sustainable garden ecosystem by choosing organic compost.

Methods of Compost Application

Applying compost isn't just tossing it on your garden beds and calling it a day. The application process is an art form that can be customized to your plants and soil needs. Here are some common methods:

- Top dressing: This technique is as straightforward as it sounds. It involves spreading a layer of compost on top of your existing soil. This is a great method for established gardens or lawns, as it allows the compost to slowly work its way into the soil, providing a steady stream of nutrients to your plants.

- Side dressing: This method is particularly useful for feeding plants during the growing season. It involves applying compost around the base of your plants, allowing the nutrients to leach into the soil where the roots can absorb them. It's like giving your plants a slow-release energy drink that keeps them growing strong.

- Compost tea: This is a potent drink for your plants. Compost tea is made by steeping compost in water, then using the nutrient-rich liquid to water your plants. This provides a quick and easily absorbable nutrient boost which is highly beneficial for plants that are struggling or need a quick pick-me-up.

Deciding on the Best Method to Apply

As I mentioned previously, deciding on the best method to apply compost to your garden largely depends on your garden's needs, your plants' needs, and the state of your soil.

For example, top dressing is an excellent all-around method that works well for most gardens. It's perfect if your plants are generally healthy and you want to keep the soil healthy long-term. This method comes in handy, especially for perennials, trees, and lawns. It offers a slow release of nutrients, enhancing soil structure over time and improving the overall health of your plants.

Side dressing is a more targeted method. If you have plants that are heavy feeders or if you're growing vegetables, this might be your best bet. Vegetables like tomatoes, peppers, and squash are nutrient hogs and will appreciate the extra boost. You can also use side dressing to boost your plants' nutrients during the growing season.

And compost tea is best used when your plants need a quick boost. If you notice that your plants are looking a little under the weather, or if they're starting out and could use a helping hand, compost tea can provide an immediate nutrient boost. It's also a fantastic way to make the most of a small amount of compost, as the tea can be diluted and used over a larger area.

Remember, though, that these methods are not mutually exclusive. You can mix and match depending on your garden's needs. Perhaps your garden beds could use some top dressing in the spring, your heavy feeders could benefit from side dressing in the summer, and a few struggling plants might appreciate a sip of compost tea.

Timing of Compost Application

Knowing when to apply compost to your garden is essential for the success of your plants. Compost can be used at any time of the year, but certain times may be more beneficial based on your garden's specific needs and the life cycle of your plants.

Most gardeners prefer to apply compost during the spring and fall, which are considered the primary composting seasons.

Spring composting is particularly beneficial as it precedes the growing season. This is when plants are just beginning to grow and can make the most of the available nutrients. Adding compost to your garden beds in early spring helps prepare the soil for new plantings. It enriches the soil with vital nutrients and beneficial microorganisms that help plants grow strong during the growing season.

On the other hand, applying compost in the fall is more about preparing for the following year. It's a great time to supplement your soil after the summer harvest has depleted nutrients. During the fall, compost has ample time to break down further and integrate with the soil. This slow, steady nourishment ensures that come spring, your garden is ready to support new growth.

In addition to these general guidelines, there are specific instances where composting can be beneficial. If you're planting a new garden bed or adding new plants, incorporating compost into the soil can give your new plants a healthy start. Similarly, during the growing season, you can side-dress plants with compost to provide an extra boost of nutrients.

Practical Tips for Compost Use

When it comes to effectively utilizing compost in your garden, there are some key strategies to follow. These practical tips help you make the most out of your compost, ensuring that it enriches your soil and benefits your plants to the maximum extent.

- Know Your Compost: Understanding the composition of your compost is key. Different compost materials have different nutrients. For example, compost made primarily from food waste will have other nutrients than compost made from yard waste.

- Turn Your Compost: Regularly turning your compost pile ensures it decomposes evenly. It also helps prevent the compost from developing a bad smell.

- Moisture Management: Your compost should be as wet as a wrung-out sponge. It won't decompose appropriately if it's too dry; if it's too wet, it can become smelly and waterlogged.

- Layer Your Compost: Layer your compost with a mix of greens (like vegetable scraps) and browns (like dry leaves). This creates a balanced compost that decomposes efficiently.

- Patience is a Virtue: Composting is a natural process that takes time. Don't rush it. A well-decomposed compost should be black, crumbly, and has a sweet earthy smell.

Common Mistakes to Avoid

As we navigate the realm of composting, it's equally crucial to acknowledge the common pitfalls that gardeners might encounter. Understanding these common mistakes can help you avoid them and ensure that your composting venture is more likely to yield successful results.

- Avoid Meat and Dairy: These can cause foul odors and attract pests. Stick to plant-based kitchen waste, yard waste, and appropriate paper products.

- Don't Use Diseased Plants: If you add plants with diseases or pests to your compost, you risk spreading the disease or pest when you use the compost.

- Avoid Overloading with One Material: Too much of one type of waste (like grass clippings) can shake off the balance of your compost.

- Don't Forget to Turn Your Compost: Neglecting to turn your compost can lead to a smelly, slow-decomposing mess.

- Avoid Synthetic Chemicals: Synthetic pesticides or fertilizers can kill beneficial organisms in your compost. Stick to organic waste for a healthy compost pile.

Success Stories from the Soil

In the realm of composting, there are many tales that can help illustrate the transformative power of this humble, natural process. Here we'll highlight a few real-life instances where compost made a huge difference.

Take, for example, the story of Susan; a city-dweller turned urban farmer. When she first began her balcony garden in the heart of the city, she struggled with poor soil and disappointing harvests. Not until she started incorporating her kitchen waste compost into her planters did her garden thrive. Her tomatoes grew larger, her herbs more flavorful, and her balcony became a green oasis amid the concrete jungle.

Then there's the tale of the Reese family. They transformed their large, barren backyard into a lush vegetable garden through composting. They created rich, fertile compost teeming with life by dedicating a corner of their yard to composting all their kitchen scraps, yard waste, and shredded paper. When they spread this compost in their garden, the results were outstanding. Their cucumber vines sprawled, their corn stalks towered, and their pumpkin patch was the talk of the neighborhood each fall.

And who could forget the story of the local community garden? To combat the declining soil quality, the community garden organizers started a communal composting program. Everyone pitched in, bringing their kitchen scraps to contribute. Over time, the compost generated was enough to revitalize the garden's soil. The result was a bountiful harvest shared among all community members, fostering a sense of unity and shared achievement.

Beyond Composting: Improve Soil Quality

O ur soil, the thin crust of earth that blankets the land, is more than just dirt. It's a living, breathing entity, replete with microscopic life and organic matter that play crucial roles in our world. The quality of this soil is integral to the health of our gardens, the food we grow, and, ultimately, our own well-being.

Understanding Soil Quality

Soil quality can be defined as the capacity of soil to function effectively as a component of a healthy ecosystem. This includes its ability to support plant life, control the flow of water, filter potential pollutants, and cycle nutrients. Healthy soil is rich in organic matter, a crucial ingredient that drives these functions.

Organic matter, derived from decomposed remnants of plants and animals, is the life force of healthy soil. It serves as the primary source of food for the myriad of microscopic organisms that inhabit the soil, promoting a rich biodiversity. In addition to nourishing plants, organic matter improves the soil's physical structure, enhancing its ability to hold and distribute water effectively.

The type of soil, determined by the relative proportions of sand, silt, and clay, also significantly influences its quality. Each type has unique characteristics, from sandy to clayey soils, and poses specific challenges and advantages for gardening. Understanding your soil type empowers you to make informed decisions about watering, plant selection, and overall soil management.

Here's a brief overview of the different types of soil:

1. Sandy Soil: Characterized by its gritty texture, sandy soil has larger particles that don't stick together, resulting in a loose structure. This allows for easy drainage but can lead to poor nutrient and water retention. It's often lighter in color and warms up quickly in the spring.

2. Silty Soil: Silty soil has smaller particles than sandy soil, resulting in a smooth, soapy texture when wet. It holds more moisture and nutrients than sandy soil, but its compact nature can hinder root growth and water drainage.

3. Clay Soil: The smallest soil particles make up clay soil, leading to a dense structure that can retain water and nutrients well. However, it can be heavy and hard to work with, mainly when dry. It's slow to warm in the spring and can cause waterlogging and poor oxygenation for plant roots.

4. Loamy Soil: Often considered the ideal garden soil, loam is a balanced mixture of sand, silt, and clay. It combines the best characteristics of the other soil types: it's nutrient-rich, has good water retention and drainage, and is easy to work with.

5. Peaty Soil: Dark and rich in organic matter, peaty soil is highly fertile. It retains a lot of water, making it soggy in wet climates but beneficial in dry ones. However, it can be acidic and may require lime to balance the pH for specific plants.

6. Chalky Soil: Chalky or alkaline soils are stony and typically found over limestone beds and chalk deposits. This soil type drains well, but many essential nutrients can be washed away. It also has a higher pH, which can make certain nutrients less available to plants.

Soil Testing and Analysis

The health of your garden is fundamentally rooted in the quality of your soil. Understanding your soil and how it can best support your plants is essential for maintaining a flourishing garden. One effective way to do this is through soil testing and analysis.

Soil testing is a way to assess the nutrient content, composition, and other characteristics of soil, such as acidity or pH level. It can provide valuable information about the current health of your soil and help you identify any deficiencies or imbalances that need to be addressed.

For amateur gardeners, there are several DIY methods for testing soil quality. One of the most common is a simple jar test to determine soil texture. This involves filling a jar with soil, adding water, shaking it, and then settling it. The different types of soil particles will separate into layers, giving you a visual representation of your soil composition.

Another DIY test involves evaluating the soil's drainage by digging a hole, filling it with water, and timing how long it takes for the water to drain. Quick drainage might mean your soil is sandy and lacking in nutrient-holding organic matter, while slow drainage could indicate heavy, compacted, or clay soil.

There are home testing kits available that can measure things like pH and nutrient levels. These kits usually involve mixing a soil sample with a testing solution or a test strip that changes color according to the properties of the soil.

For a more comprehensive analysis, you can consider professional soil testing services. These services utilize advanced techniques to provide a detailed report on various soil properties, including nutrient content, pH level, organic matter content, and more. While this option might be a bit more costly, it can give you an in-depth understanding of your soil's health.

Once you've conducted your soil test, the next step is interpreting the results. This might seem daunting initially, but remember that the goal is to better understand your soil to guide your gardening practices. If your soil is too acidic or alkaline, you might need to add certain amendments to adjust the pH. If your soil is lacking in certain nutrients, you might need to add a specific type of fertilizer or compost.

Techniques for Improving Soil Quality

Improving soil health is not a one-time effort but a continuous process of nurturing and maintaining balance. Various techniques can be adopted to enhance soil quality beyond composting. These methods are all about working with nature to create rich, healthy soil that will nourish your plants and help your garden thrive. Let's look at some of these techniques:

1. Crop Rotation: This practice is typically associated with large-scale farming but can also be adapted for home gardens. The idea is to change the type of plant grown in each area of your garden each season. For example, if you grow tomatoes (which are heavy feeders) one year, consider planting beans (which are light feeders and nitrogen fixers) in that spot the following year. This prevents the build-up of specific plant diseases and pests and allows the soil to replenish its nutrients.

2. Cover Crops: Also known as green manure, cover crops are plants grown specifically to improve soil health. They help to increase organic matter, protect against erosion, boost soil structure, and suppress weeds. Some common cover crops for home gardens include clover, field peas, and buckwheat. Once they've grown, they can be cut down and left on the soil surface to decompose or be tilled into the soil.

3. Mulching: Mulch serves many functions in the garden. It helps to retain soil moisture, reduces weeds, and as it breaks down, it adds organic matter to the soil. Organic mulches can include straw, shredded leaves, or wood chips. Remember to replenish your mulch as it decomposes throughout the season.

4. Use of Organic Fertilizers: Organic fertilizers are derived from plant or animal sources and contain essential nutrients for plant growth. They release their nutrients slowly, feeding your plants and improving the overall fertility of your soil. Examples of organic fertilizers include bone meal, blood meal, fish emulsion, and kelp meal.

5. Adding Beneficial Microorganisms: Some gardeners choose to add beneficial soil microorganisms, such as mycorrhizal fungi or compost tea, to their soil to help improve nutrient absorption and enhance soil health. You can find them in gardening stores and add them to your soil following the package instructions.

Remember, every garden is unique, and what works best will depend on your specific soil conditions and the plants you are growing.

Soil Amendments and Their Applications

Entering the realm of soil amendments, you'll uncover an arsenal of garden-enhancing tools. These not-so-secret ingredients can turn your soil from just fine to garden gold. They are gardeners' best friends, modifying your soil to create the perfect cozy home for your plants.

Among our crew of soil amendments, we have lime, sulfur, and gypsum, each bringing its unique talent to the garden party. Just as the perfect spice mix elevates a humble dish, the suitable amendment can make your garden bloom like never before.

For instance, lime is the go-to amendment when dealing with acid-loving soils. It raises the pH making the soil more alkaline, which is a preferred environment for many plants. On the other hand, sulfur is the hero for soils with high alkalinity, helping lower the pH to a more balanced level. Gypsum is the handyman of soil amendments, remedying compacted soils and making it more hospitable for root expansion and water penetration.

However, knowing the what and why of soil amendments is just the start. The real charm lies in learning how to use them effectively.

- Understand your soil: Test your soil to know its pH and structure. Does it need lime or sulfur? Or maybe gypsum? This knowledge is crucial in deciding which amendment it needs.

- Blend, don't just sprinkle: Mix the amendments into the soil for an even spread. This ensures the nutrients are accessible to the plant roots.

Now that you know the correct way, let's examine some common pitfalls to avoid:

1. Over-amending: Too much of anything is bad, which also holds true for soil amendments. Excessive amendments can result in nutrient imbalances that harm your plants rather than help them.

2. Using the wrong amendment: Not every amendment suits every soil. Adding lime to an already alkaline soil or sulfur to an acidic one does more harm than good.

3. Expecting instant results: Good things take time, and soil amendments are no exception. Be patient and allow the amendments to work their magic.

Soil amendments are the final brushstrokes to a beautiful garden canvas, fine-tuning your soil to the needs of your plants. Remember, they're not a one-step solution but a part of your broader gardening strategy. They complete your composting efforts, fostering a vibrant ecosystem.

Compost Tea: Boosting Plant Health with Liquid Gold

C ompost Tea. What does it remind you of? Unlike its cozy name, compost tea isn't sipped from a teacup on a rainy afternoon. It's a garden super-drink, a potent brew that turns your garden into a wonderland of lush plant life. Picture your garden flourishing with radiant, healthy plants, all thanks to the 'liquid gold' that is compost tea. So, raise your watering can to a toast for thriving gardens!

Compost tea is essentially a liquid extraction full of beneficial microorganisms that come from compost. It's created by steeping compost in water, like preparing a regular cup of tea, but you get a nutrient-rich brew that provides an easy-to-absorb source of nutrition for your plants.

The magic of compost tea lies not only in its nutrient content but also in its ability to suppress diseases, enhance plant growth, and improve the quality of your crops. This concentrated solution doesn't just boost plant health; it also contributes to improving soil structure, making it an invaluable ally for any gardener aiming to cultivate a prosperous garden.

The Science Behind Compost Tea

Unraveling the magic of compost tea involves understanding the key elements that bring its power to fruition. This brew is more than just a steeped compost pile; it's a potent concoction teaming with microorganisms that aid plant growth and disease suppression. Here, we'll dissect the components that make compost tea the liquid gold it's often called.

- Beneficial Microorganisms: The primary contributors to the effectiveness of compost tea are beneficial microorganisms. These tiny powerhouses, including bacteria, fungi, and protozoa, are derived from the compost used to brew tea. When applied to the plants or soil, they work to break down organic matter into essential nutrients that the plants can readily absorb. They significantly enhance soil and plant health, operating quietly behind the scenes.

- Nutrient-Rich Solution: The compost tea brewing process involves steeping compost in water, allowing the beneficial microbes to multiply and creating a concentrated, nutrient-dense solution. This "liquid gold" is teeming with the necessary nutrients plants need to thrive, making it a potent elixir.

- Disease Suppression: One of the main advantages of compost tea is its ability to suppress plant diseases. The beneficial microbes in the tea compete with disease-causing organisms, effectively reducing their numbers and preventing the onset of disease.

- Soil Health and Structure: Besides providing plant nutrients, compost tea also benefits the soil. Applying compost tea improves soil, boosts its nutrient content, and enhances its ability to retain moisture.

- Plant Growth Enhancement: Studies have shown that compost tea can enhance plant growth. The beneficial microbes in the tea help make nutrients more available to plants, leading to healthier, stronger, and more productive growth.

Materials Needed

Compost

Not just any compost, but high-quality, well-aged compost. This elixir carries the beneficial microbes we aim to multiply in our tea. You can create your own compost at home from kitchen scraps, yard waste, and other organic materials, or you can buy it from a local garden store. Either way, the quality of your compost will significantly impact the potency of your compost tea, so choose wisely.

Water (ideally chlorine-free)

Now, you might be thinking, "Water, got it. I can just fill up a bucket from the tap, right?" Well, not quite. The water you use should ideally be free of chlorine, as chlorine can kill the very microbes we're trying to cultivate in our compost tea. If you're using tap water, let it sit out in an open container for 24 hours before using it. This allows the chlorine to evaporate. Alternatively, you can use rainwater or distilled water.

A compost tea brewer or a bucket

The size of your brewing container will depend on the volume of tea you intend to make. A five-gallon bucket is usually sufficient for home gardeners. If you're getting serious about this and want to make larger batches, consider investing in a compost tea brewer, explicitly designed for this purpose and often comes with features that facilitate the brewing process. But remember, if you're just starting out, a simple, clean bucket will do the trick.

An air pump (for aeration)

You might wonder, "Why must I aerate my compost tea?" The answer lies in the nature of the beneficial microbes we're trying to cultivate. Many of these are aerobic, meaning they thrive in the presence of oxygen. Aeration promotes the growth of these beneficial aerobic microbes while discouraging the growth of potentially harmful anaerobic ones. For this reason, you'll need an air pump, similar to what's used in fish tanks, to infuse your compost tea with oxygen throughout the brewing process.

Aeration stones (optional)

These handy little tools, also known as air stones or diffusers, are connected to the air pump and placed at the bottom of your brewing container. They break up the air pumped into the water into tiny bubbles, maximizing the oxygenation of your compost tea and promoting the growth of our much-desired microbes.

Strainer or cheesecloth

After brewing, you must separate the liquid compost tea from the solid compost particles. This is where the strainer or cheesecloth comes in. A strainer with a fine mesh is ideal, as it allows you to capture even the smallest particles. Cheesecloth also works well and has the added benefit of being washable and reusable.

Unsulfured molasses (optional)

Molasses provides sugars that feed the microbial population, encouraging their growth and multiplication. This is an optional ingredient but can be beneficial as a food source for the microbes in your compost tea. Ensure the molasses is unsulfured, as sulfur can potentially harm our beneficial microbes.

Making Your Own Compost Tea

Alright, we've got our tools and materials ready, so it's time to roll up our sleeves and get our hands into the compost! It's also time to set the stage for our little microbial actors, creating the perfect environment for them to put on the performance of a lifetime in the form of rich, nutritious compost tea.

In the first act of this grand performance, we need to prepare our compost. Choosing high-quality, well-aged compost is critical, because it forms the foundation of your compost tea. This compost should be rich in organic material, relatively dark in color, and have a pleasant earthy smell. If you're making your own compost at home, ensure it's fully decomposed and aged before using it for your tea. If you're buying compost, opt for a trusted brand or source to ensure it's of high quality.

The quantity of compost needed will depend on the size of your brewer and the volume of tea you want to make. A general rule of thumb is to use a ratio of 1 part compost to 5 parts water. So, for a 5-gallon bucket, you'd use about 1 gallon of compost. Remember, it's not about packing in as much compost as possible, but about creating a balanced environment for our microbial stars to shine.

Now that we have our compost ready, let's turn to setting up the brewer, the stage where all the magic happens. Start by positioning the air pump and aeration stones, if you're using them. The air pump should be set up outside the brewer and the aeration stones placed at the bottom of the brewer. Ensure the pump is connected to a reliable power source, and the stones are properly attached to the pump via the air tubing.

COMPOST TEA

NYLON STOCKING

COMPOST

PLASTIC TUBING

AIR STONE

AQUARIUM PUMP

Once the air pump and stones are in place, fill the brewer with water. Remember, we want chlorine-free water, so if you're using tap water, be sure it's been dechlorinated.

Now, add the compost to the brewer. You can put the compost directly into the water, or, to make the straining process easier later on, you can put the compost in a permeable bag (like a large tea bag) and place that in the water.

Now that our brewer is ready, it's time to move on to the main act - the brewing process itself.

Begin by starting the air pump. This sets the stage for our aerobic microbes, supplying them with the oxygen they need to thrive. You should see bubbles rising through the water, indicating that the aeration process is working. This step is crucial, as it promotes the growth of beneficial microbes and prevents the brew from turning anaerobic, which could result in the growth of harmful bacteria.

If you've chosen to use unsulfured molasses, now's the time to add it to the mix. The molasses serves as a food source for the microbes, encouraging their growth and multiplication. You typically want to add about 1-2 tablespoons of molasses per gallon of water. Stir the brew gently to ensure the molasses is evenly distributed.

Next, we let nature take its course. The brew time for compost tea is typically between 24 to 48 hours. During this time, the microbes in the compost will feed on the organic matter and multiply, creating a rich, nutrient-dense tea. Keep an eye on the brew during this period; it should have a pleasant, earthy smell, indicative of healthy microbial activity. If it starts to smell foul, something's gone awry, and it's best to start over.

Finally, once your compost tea has brewed, it's time for the closing act - the post-brewing process. Using your strainer or cheesecloth, strain the compost tea to separate the liquid from the solid compost particles. This leaves you with a smooth, particle-free tea that's ready to be used in your garden.

What to do with the used compost? Don't throw it away! It's still rich in nutrients and can be added back to your compost pile or used as a soil amendment in your garden.

The compost tea itself can be used in a variety of ways. It can be applied directly to the soil as a soil drench, or used as a foliar spray on the leaves of your plants. When used regularly, compost tea can enhance soil fertility, boost plant health, and help create a vibrant, productive garden.

How and When to Use Compost Tea

Compost tea can transform your garden into a green haven when applied correctly and timely, like a special secret ingredient in a gardener's arsenal.

When it comes to using compost tea, flexibility is vital. It can be applied in two ways: as a soil drench or a foliar spray. A soil drench involves simply pouring the compost tea directly onto the soil around your plants. This method enriches the soil with beneficial microorganisms, improving soil structure and nutrient content. On the other hand, a foliar spray means spraying the compost tea directly onto the leaves of your plants. This technique allows the plants to absorb the nutrients quickly, boosting their immune system and making them less susceptible to diseases.

Timing is another crucial aspect when using compost tea. While you can use it anytime during the growing season, certain times can maximize its effectiveness. For instance, applying compost tea at the onset of your planting season can give your plants a healthy start. You can also consider using it when your plants are under stress or when they are flowering or fruiting, as they require an extra nutrient boost during these times.

Lastly, it's essential to use your compost tea promptly after brewing, ideally within a few hours, to harness the power of the living microorganisms. Keep in mind that compost tea is a living solution; the longer it sits, the less effective it becomes.

Troubleshooting and FAQs

Here are some troubleshooting tips and answers to frequently asked questions (FAQs):

- Compost Tea Smells Bad: If your compost tea has a foul smell, it may be anaerobic. This issue can occur due to a lack of aeration during the brewing process or the compost used wasn't fully decomposed. It's best to discard smelly compost tea, as it may contain harmful pathogens.

- Foam in Compost Tea: Some foam is normal during the brewing process due to the activity of beneficial microbes. However, the excessive foam could indicate too much food source (like molasses) for the microbes.

- Best Water for Brewing Compost Tea: It's best to use dechlorinated water for brewing compost tea, as chlorine can kill beneficial microbes. If you only have access to chlorinated tap water, let it sit out for 24 hours to allow the chlorine to evaporate before using it to brew your tea.

- Frequency of Application: Compost tea can be applied as often as once a week during the growing season. However, more isn't always better. Observe your plants and apply when they need a nutrient boost, like during blooming or periods of stress.

- Using Compost Tea on All Plants: Yes, compost tea can be used on all types of plants, including vegetables, flowers, shrubs, trees, and lawns. It's a natural, non-toxic way to enhance plant health.

- Storing Compost Tea: As I said, compost tea is a living solution and is best used immediately after brewing. If you must store it, do so in a cool, dark place and use it within 24-48 hours.

- Compost Tea vs. Commercial Fertilizers: While commercial fertilizers can provide a quick nutrient boost, compost tea enriches the soil with beneficial microorganisms, leading to improved soil health and structure over time.

Crop Rotation: Planning for Long-Term Soil Health

I n the vibrant world of sustainable gardening, composting and crop rotation are steadfast friends, nurturing and caring for our precious soil. Let's uncover the magic of their partnership, a dynamic duo that takes your garden soil's health from fleeting to long-lasting.

Compost, the nutrient-rich humus created from decomposed organic material, is like a multivitamin for the soil. It contributes essential nutrients, augments the soil's structure, enhances its moisture retention capacity, and promotes a thriving community of beneficial soil organisms.

Parallelly, crop rotation is the strategic practice of changing the type of crop grown in a particular area in sequential seasons. This agricultural tradition checks disease and pest patterns, preserves soil fertility, and effectively manages nutrient consumption and replenishment. The nourishment provided by compost energizes the soil, while crop rotation safeguards this vitality, ensuring soil health in the long run.

Understanding Crop Rotation

In the grand canvas of agriculture, crop rotation paints a picture of sustainability, balance, and foresight. Simply put, crop rotation is an age-old farming practice in which different types of crops are planted in the same area over sequential seasons. Imagine a farmer's field as a stage, where different crops take turns to play their part in an ongoing agricultural performance. By allowing various crops to take center stage at different times, the soil's health and the farming system's overall resilience are maintained.

Why is this rotation so important? Each type of crop interacts with the soil and the environment in unique ways, much like different actors bringing their own flavor to a performance. Some crops, like legumes, are known as 'nitrogen fixers.' They have the impressive ability to convert atmospheric nitrogen into a form that plants can use, effectively enriching the soil with this essential nutrient. Conversely, other crops are 'heavy feeders,' drawing substantial amounts of specific nutrients from the soil. By alternating between these different types of crops, farmers can ensure that the soil's nutrient balance is maintained and that it doesn't get exhausted from continuously catering to the same demands.

To illustrate this concept, let's take an example of a small farm in rural Nebraska. Farmer Jane, a savvy cultivator, knows the value of crop rotation. After growing a season of corn, a heavy nitrogen feeder, she plants soybeans, a legume, the following season. The soybeans replenish the soil's nitrogen levels that the corn had depleted, maintaining the soil's nutrient balance and ensuring that it's ready for the next cycle of corn or other nitrogen-loving crops.

The benefits of crop rotation extend far beyond just nutrient management. Here's a list to provide a more holistic understanding:

1. Improving Soil Fertility: As already discussed, alternating between different types of crops can help maintain and improve the soil's nutrient balance.

2. Pest and Disease Control: Different crops attract different pests and diseases. Farmers can disrupt the life cycles of these pests and diseases by rotating crops, reducing their populations and impact.

3. Weed Management: Some crops, like potatoes, can help suppress weeds by shading the soil with their dense foliage, reducing the need for labor-intensive weeding.

4. Promoting Biodiversity: A diverse range of crops can support various beneficial insects, birds, and other wildlife, enhancing the farm's overall ecological health.

5. Preventing Soil Erosion: Certain crops, especially those with deep roots, can help hold the soil together, preventing erosion by wind and water.

6. Enhancing Soil Structure: Different crops have different root structures, and by rotating crops, the soil structure can be improved, promoting better water infiltration and root growth.

Types of Crops in Rotation

In the world of agriculture, not all crops are created equal. Each crop type belongs to a particular family and exhibits unique characteristics, including specific nutrient needs and benefits to the soil and environment. Just like family members share certain traits and features, so do crops within the same botanical family. Understanding these crop families and their specific needs and benefits is crucial when planning a crop rotation scheme. So, let's delve deeper into some key crop families and their individual quirks and features.

Legumes: The Nitrogen Fixers

Consider the legume family, which includes peas, beans, lentils, and even peanuts. These plants have a remarkable ability to form a symbiotic relationship with bacteria in their root nodules, allowing them to "fix" nitrogen from the atmosphere and convert it into a form that plants can use. This makes legumes the natural fertilizers of the plant world. They're the stars of any crop rotation program, leaving the soil richer than they found it.

Imagine a humble pea plant, sprouting in a field where a heavy-feeding crop like corn was harvested the previous season. As it grows, the pea plant works in harmony with the bacteria in its roots, replenishing the soil with precious nitrogen, and preparing the stage for the next crop in the rotation. It's a silent, yet essential, process that occurs beneath the soil, largely unseen but absolutely vital for the health of the soil and the success of future crops.

Brassicas: The Heavy Feeders

Then, we have the Brassica family, which includes crops like cabbage, broccoli, kale, and cauliflower. These plants are what we call 'heavy feeders.' They have a voracious appetite for nutrients, especially nitrogen, and can deplete the soil if grown continuously. However, they also play an essential role in crop rotation. By following a nitrogen-fixing legume crop with a nitrogen-loving Brassica, farmers can effectively utilize the nitrogen added to the soil by the legumes.

Picture a robust cabbage plant, its wide leaves spread out to catch the sunlight, thriving in soil rich in nitrogen left behind by the previous season's bean crop. It's a testament to the power of crop rotation, a system where one plant's waste is another plant's treasure.

Alliums: The Light Feeders

Finally, let's turn our attention to the Allium family, which includes onions, garlic, leeks, and shallots. These plants are generally considered 'light feeders.' They require fewer nutrients than heavy feeders like Brassicas and can be effectively grown in soil previously used by more nutrient-demanding crops. Alliums also have the added benefit of deterring certain pests with their strong scent, providing natural pest control.

Imagine a row of garlic plants, their slender leaves reaching for the sky, growing in soil once home to a crop of nutrient-hungry broccoli. The soil might be less nutrient-rich than before, but that's perfect for these light-feeding garlic plants. Their strong aroma keeps many pests at bay, adding another layer of protection for the crops to follow in the rotation.

Planning Your Crop Rotation

A well-planned crop rotation is like a well-orchestrated symphony. Each crop plays its part, contributing to the overall performance and harmony of the system. Planning your crop rotation involves considering several factors, including the number of crop rotation groups, the characteristics of each crop, and the basic rules of crop rotation.

Determining the Number of Crop Rotation Groups

The first step in planning your crop rotation is determining the number of crop rotation groups. This is largely dependent on the space you have available. In an ideal world, with unlimited space, you could have many crop rotation groups, allowing for a diverse range of crops and a long rotation period.

However, in reality, space can often be a limiting factor. If you only have a small garden, you might only be able to manage two or three crop rotation groups. Let's take the example of a beginner gardener, John, who only has a small backyard plot. He decides to divide his plot into three sections, allowing for a simple three-year crop rotation with legumes, Brassicas, and Alliums.

Considering Crop Characteristics

Next, you need to consider the characteristics of each crop. This includes their growth period (how long they need to be in the ground), nutrient requirements, and susceptibility to common pests or diseases.

For instance, some crops, like radishes, are fast-growing and can be harvested within a month, while others, like garlic, need to be in the ground for several months. Some crops, like Brassicas, are heavy feeders, requiring lots of nutrients, while others, like Alliums, are lighter feeders. Similarly, some crops are susceptible to certain pests or diseases, which should not be followed by other crops susceptible to the same issues.

Understanding the Basic Rules of Crop Rotation

Finally, it's essential to understand the basic rules of crop rotation. These rules are not hard and fast laws but guiding principles that can help you make effective decisions.

One of the fundamental rules is to avoid following crops from the same family. Crops from the same family tend to have similar nutrient requirements and are often susceptible to the same pests and diseases. By rotating crops from different families, you can help to maintain soil fertility and reduce pest and disease pressure.

Another rule is to consider the nutrient needs of each crop. As a general guide, following a heavy-feeding crop with a light-feeding crop or a nitrogen-fixing legume crop with a nitrogen-loving crop is often beneficial.

For instance, let's return to our friend John with his three-sectioned garden. In the first year, he could plant peas (a legume) in the first section, broccoli (a heavy feeder) in the second, and onions (a light feeder) in the third. The following year, he could rotate the crops, moving the peas to the second section (where they can replenish the nitrogen taken up by the previous year's broccoli), the broccoli to the third section (where it can benefit from the residual fertility), and the onions to the first section (where they can thrive even as the nutrient levels are lower).

In the next section, we'll take this plan from paper to soil, discussing how to implement your crop rotation and nurture your crops from seed to harvest. Remember, a thriving crop rotation is not just about the right plan, but also about careful implementation, observation, and adjustment.

Implementing Your Crop Rotation

After thoughtful planning, it's time to roll up your sleeves and bring your crop rotation plan to life. The implementation process involves understanding your soil, creating a visual guide, and finally, planting your crops. While it may initially seem challenging, remember that every step brings you closer to a sustainable and bountiful garden.

Starting with a Soil Test

Think of soil testing as a health check-up for your garden. A soil test provides valuable insights into your soil's current nutrient composition, guiding your crop rotation decisions. It uncovers the levels of essential nutrients, like nitrogen, phosphorus, and potassium, along with the soil's pH.

For instance, let's consider Maria, a novice gardener. She's excited to start her vegetable garden and has researched crop rotation. Before diving in, she decides to conduct a soil test. The results reveal a high nitrogen content, which is excellent news for her nitrogen-loving crops, like Brassicas. However, she understands the importance of balancing her soil nutrition through crop rotation to avoid over-depleting nutrients.

Creating a Crop Rotation Map

Once you understand your soil, the next step is to create a crop rotation map. This map is a visual guide that outlines where each crop will go in the rotation for each year.

Consider a small-scale organic farmer, David. He has four fields at his disposal and decides to implement a four-year crop rotation plan. He sketches a simple diagram of his fields, marking each one as Field A, B, C, and D. For the first year, he decides to plant legumes in Field A, Brassicas in Field B, root crops in Field C, and Alliums in Field D. For the next year, he plans to rotate his crops, with each crop moving one field to the right. His map is a visual guide that will aid him throughout his crop rotation journey.

Planting Your Crops According to the Plan

The final step is to plant your crops according to your plan. This is where all your preparation and planning come to fruition.

Let's return to our friend Maria, who, armed with her soil test results and a crop rotation map, is ready to start planting. She's planned a simple three-year rotation with legumes, Brassicas, and Alliums. Following her map, she plants peas in the first section of her garden, broccoli in the second, and onions in the third. She knows that sticking to her plan is crucial for the success of her crop rotation.

Monitoring and Adjusting Your Crop Rotation

Implementing your crop rotation plan is only part of the journey. The process doesn't end once the seeds are in the ground. Instead, it continues through careful monitoring and periodic adjustments to ensure your soil's health and your crops' success.

Keeping Records

The first step towards effective monitoring is keeping thorough records. This involves tracking what was planted, where and when, and any problems encountered.

Let's consider Lisa, an amateur gardener who's just started with her three-year crop rotation plan. Lisa understands the value of record-keeping and maintains a garden diary. In this diary, she meticulously notes each crop's planting and harvesting dates, the pests she encountered, and the measures she took to control them. She also records her observations on crop growth and yield.

Adjusting Your Plan Based on Observations

As you gain experience and learn more about your garden, you may need to adjust your crop rotation plan based on your observations and results.

For instance, suppose Lisa notices that her Brassicas aren't growing as well as she had hoped in one part of her garden. She might decide to swap the position of her Brassicas and legumes in the next year's rotation, believing that the legumes' nitrogen-fixing capabilities might better serve that area of her garden.

Re-Testing Your Soil

Finally, re-testing your soil every few years is crucial in understanding how your rotation impacts the soil's nutrient composition.

Let's say that after three years of her crop rotation plan, Lisa decides to conduct another soil test. The results show a balanced nutrient composition, a testament to her thoughtful and well-implemented crop rotation. However, she notices a slight dip in phosphorus levels. Based on this, she decides to incorporate crops like beans and peas, known to help increase soil phosphorus, into her rotation more frequently.

Role of Compost in Crop Rotation

Compost is a crucial supplement in crop rotation, replenishing soil nutrients and enhancing soil structure. As we know, compost is like a multivitamin for your soil, packed with essential nutrients and beneficial microorganisms. In this chapter, we'll explore how to incorporate compost into your crop rotation plan and the benefits it can bring to your garden.

Let's take the example of Sarah, an urban gardener, who has set up a small compost bin in her backyard. She adds kitchen scraps like coffee grounds and vegetable peelings and yard waste like fallen leaves and grass clippings. Over time, these materials decompose and transform into rich, dark compost, teeming with nutrients ready to nourish her garden.

Incorporating Compost into Crop Rotation

One common approach is adding compost before planting a heavy-feeding crop, such as Brassica family members. These nutrient-hungry plants can take advantage of the nutrient boost provided by the compost.

For instance, Sarah might add a layer of her homemade compost to the section of her garden where she plans to plant her broccoli. The compost enriches the soil with nutrients, setting the stage for her broccoli plants to thrive.

Benefits of Compost in Crop Rotation

Incorporating compost into your crop rotation helps replenish nutrients in the soil, improves soil structure and water retention, and promotes the activity of beneficial soil organisms.

Moreover, compost can help mitigate some of the challenges of crop rotation. For example, suppose Sarah notices that a particular section of her garden isn't performing well despite rotating her crops. In that case, she might add more compost to improve the soil's fertility and structure.

Troubleshooting Common Issues

In your journey through crop rotation, you may encounter some challenges. However, equipped with knowledge and understanding, you can navigate through these issues effectively. Let's address some common questions and problems in crop rotation, such as dealing with persistent pests or diseases and nutrient deficiencies.

1. Persistent Pests or Diseases

Even with a well-planned crop rotation, you might still encounter persistent pests or diseases. If you notice the same pest or disease issue recurring year after year, even though you're rotating your crops, it might be time to introduce a different crop family into the rotation or extend the rotation period. By introducing greater diversity or allowing more time between plantings of the same crop family, you can help break the pest or disease cycle.

2. Nutrient Deficiencies

If you notice signs of nutrient deficiencies in your plants, such as yellowing leaves or stunted growth, it might be a sign that your soil needs a nutrient boost. Depending on the specific deficiency, you might need to adjust your crop rotation to include more of a certain type of crop (like nitrogen-fixing legumes for nitrogen deficiency) or consider adding organic matter or other soil amendments to replenish the nutrients.

3. Poor Crop Performance

If a crop isn't performing as well as expected, it could be due to a variety of factors. Maybe the crop isn't suited to your specific climate or soil type, or perhaps it was planted at the wrong time of year. This is where keeping detailed records can be particularly helpful. By reviewing your records, you can identify patterns and make informed adjustments to your rotation plan.

4. Limited Space

For those working with limited space, it can be challenging to implement a diverse crop rotation. In such cases, you might need to get creative. Consider vertical gardening methods to maximize space or using containers for some crops. You might also focus on rotating between just a few key crop families, prioritizing those that have shown the best results in your garden.

5. Weather Challenges

Weather conditions, such as drought or excessive rainfall, can also pose challenges. If you're facing a drought, consider incorporating more drought-tolerant crops into your rotation. If you're dealing with excessive rain, focus on crops that can handle wetter conditions or consider improving your soil's drainage.

Further Practices for Long-Term Soil Health

While composting and crop rotation are fundamental to sustainable gardening, there are additional straightforward techniques you can apply to further enhance your soil health. Here are some beginner-friendly practices you can adopt:

- Companion Planting: This involves growing certain plants together for their mutual benefit. For example, tomatoes, basil, and marigolds are often planted together because they support each other's growth and deter pests.

- Cover Cropping: Planting cover crops, such as clover or rye, can protect your soil from erosion, suppress weeds, and enhance soil fertility. Once they're done growing, they can be left to decompose on the surface or be dug into the soil.

- Mulching: Mulching involves covering the soil surface with organic materials like straw, leaves, or wood chips. This can help conserve moisture, suppress weeds, and improve soil structure and fertility as the mulch decomposes.

- Use of Organic Fertilizers: In addition to compost, other organic fertilizers such as bone meal, fish emulsion, or worm castings can provide different nutrients to the soil and promote plant health.

- Rainwater Harvesting: Collecting and using rainwater for irrigation is another sustainable practice that can contribute to a more prosperous garden. Rainwater is typically more beneficial for plants than tap water.

These techniques are easy to implement and can substantially benefit soil health. As with composting and crop rotation, the key is consistency and patience.

BOOK VI

COMPOST AND SUSTAINABILITY

NURTURING OUR PLANET
THROUGH CONSCIOUS LIVING

The choices we make today will profoundly influence the quality of life for future generations. In a world where our actions increasingly impact the environment, we must choose a more sustainable lifestyle.

And within our spectrum of choices, composting emerges as a powerful ally in our journey toward sustainability.

The Role of Composting in Sustainable Living

Composting, in its unassuming yet powerful simplicity, is an ode to nature's cyclical rhythms. This transformative process paints a captivating picture of renewal, transforming seemingly little scraps - food remains, foliage, or grass trimmings - into a vibrant, life-sustaining resource. This nutrient-laden compost enriches the soil, minimizes reliance on manufactured fertilizers, and bolsters the growth of sturdy, flourishing flora.

In essence, composting offers a miniature yet potent representation of the larger aspiration of eco-friendly living. It manifests core principles like resource optimization, waste minimization, and circularity, embodying a harmonious dance between creation and decay, growth and return. Composting, therefore, transcends the pragmatic task of garden nourishment. It invites us to embrace a worldview that esteems sustainability and resonates with the inherent cyclical cadence of Mother Earth.

Environmental Benefits of Composting

Have you ever thought about the profound impact our daily habits can have on the planet? Let me tell you that simple actions, like composting our kitchen scraps and garden waste, can collectively make a significant difference. By understanding the environmental benefits of composting, we can better appreciate its value and feel even more motivated to make it a part of our green lifestyle. Now, let's explore these benefits in detail.

One of the standout benefits of composting is its power to reduce landfill waste. It might surprise you that around 30% of household waste comprises organic materials - think vegetable peels, coffee grounds, eggshells, and yard clippings. These items could be composted right at home, transformed into nutrient-rich soil amendment instead of being thrown into the trash. By composting, you actively minimize the amount of waste that ends up in landfills. This has a ripple effect - less waste means fewer resources are needed for waste transport and processing, and we keep organic materials out of landfills where they decompose and release methane, which is a potent greenhouse gas.

Composting doesn't just reduce landfill waste - it also helps decrease greenhouse gas emissions. When organic waste is dumped into a landfill, it decomposes in an oxygen-poor environment, releasing methane. In contrast, composting at home is an aerobic process, meaning it occurs in the presence of oxygen. This aerobic decomposition produces far less greenhouse gases, making it a much greener approach.

Another feather in composting's cap is its role in conserving natural resources. When you use compost in your garden or for your plants, you add a powerhouse of nutrients to the soil. This nutrient boost substantially decreases the need for synthetic fertilizers. Compost also improves soil structure, allowing it to absorb water more effectively and lowering the necessity for regular irrigation. By integrating compost into your gardening routine, you're nurturing your plants while conserving resources, a win-win situation!

Beyond its direct benefits to your garden, compost also contributes to preserving biodiversity. A healthy, compost-enriched soil is a suitable habitat for a diverse range of organisms. From beneficial insects to microorganisms, creatures that contribute significantly to the health of our broader ecosystem. Your compost heap is, in fact, a little biodiversity hotspot, playing a small but crucial role in supporting life.

Finally, composting aids in carbon sequestration, capturing and storing atmospheric carbon dioxide. Composting captures carbon and locks it away in the compost itself. When you add this compost to the soil, you effectively store this carbon in the ground, preventing it from going back to the atmosphere.

Economic Advantages of Composting

In addition to the significant environmental advantages of composting, there are also real economic benefits. These can often be overlooked, yet are another compelling reason to consider adopting composting as part of a more sustainable lifestyle.

One of the best ways composting can save you money is by minimizing the need to purchase synthetic fertilizers. When you compost, you are creating a rich, nutrient-dense product that can be used to feed your plants and enrich your garden's soil. This "black gold," as gardeners often call compost, is a natural and highly effective fertilizer you're producing for free from your kitchen scraps and yard waste.

By regularly adding compost to your garden, you'll find that the overall soil health and fertility improve over time. Healthy, fertile soil is the foundation of a thriving garden that needs fewer other gardening products, such as soil amendments or conditioners.

Additionally, as compost improves your soil structure, your garden will become more efficient at retaining water. This means you'll have to spend less time and money watering. It also means your plants will be more resilient during periods of drought, potentially saving you the cost of replacing plants that might not survive these challenging conditions.

Let's not forget about the potential savings in waste management. In many areas, households have to pay for waste collection services. By composting, you reduce the amount of waste that needs to be collected, which could potentially lead to savings, especially if your municipality charges based on the amount of waste you produce.

Finally, composting can save you money on purchasing produce by making your garden more productive and resilient. If you're composting for a vegetable garden, over time, you might find that you can grow more of your own food, reducing the money you spend at the grocery store.

When we view composting through the lens of economic benefits, it's clear that this practice can be a wise financial decision. It's an investment in the health of your garden and the health of our planet. As with all the best investments, the returns make the effort well worth it.

Composting and Regenerative Agriculture

As we continue to strive for more sustainable ways of living, the role of composting takes on increasing significance. Here we'll try to look at composting not merely as a waste management strategy but as a vital component of regenerative agriculture—a practice designed to work in harmony with nature to restore the health of our ecosystem. Below are some important points that highlight how composting fits into larger sustainable agricultural practices and the concept of a circular economy:

1. Promoting Soil Life: Composting is crucial for promoting life within the soil, for it introduces beneficial organisms that aid in the breakdown of organic matter, converting it into accessible plant nutrients.

2. Cycling of Nutrients: When it comes to a circular economy, composting

aids in recycling nutrients back into the ecosystem. Nutrients that would otherwise be lost as waste are returned to the soil, supporting plant growth and reducing the need for synthetic fertilizers.

3. Reducing Erosion: Healthy soil, bolstered by compost, is less prone to erosion. By improving the soil structure, compost helps minimize soil degradation, a fundamental principle of sustainable agriculture.

4. Adapting to Climate Change: Composting is a part of sustainable farming practices that help adapt to climate change. Improving soil's water-holding capacity helps in dealing with water scarcity and drought issues.

5. Community Engagement: On a community level, composting initiatives can engage people in sustainable practices, raising awareness of waste management, food systems, and their environmental impact.

6. Biofuel Production: Composting can be integrated into systems that produce biofuel, a renewable form of energy. A composting method known as anaerobic digestion, for example, creates biogas. This not only turns waste into valuable energy but also aligns with the principles of a circular economy, a system aimed at minimizing waste and making the most of the resources at our disposal.

Spreading the Compost Revolution

In the world of composting, advocacy stands as our most potent instrument. Picture this: a cascading wave of change that begins with a single individual – who can be YOU - and then radiates outward, influencing your friends, relatives, neighbors and even extending to broader communities.

In the same way, compost transforms scraps into nutrient-rich soil; advocacy has the potential to transform individuals into agents of change. Just as a single seed can grow into a lush tree, so can the actions of one person inspire a whole community, helping it flourish. This is the essence of advocacy in composting: taking our knowledge and passion and spreading it around like compost in a garden, fostering growth wherever possible.

Let's explore together how we can use advocacy to its fullest, taking the compost revolution far and wide, one enlightening conversation at a time.

Grassroots Movements and Composting

Riding the wave of grassroots movements, composting has found a strong ally in these community-led initiatives. These movements have illustrated the transformative power of community engagement, turning kitchen scraps and yard waste into black gold for their local gardens. Their humble beginnings rooted in local neighborhoods have proven that the journey toward sustainability starts right at home.

Take the example of the "Compost Queens" in San Antonio, Texas. This mother-daughter duo started a community composting service that reduces waste and provides rich compost to local farms and gardens. Both sides stand to gain - community members have a simple way to reduce their waste, and local agriculture benefits from nutrient-rich compost.

Across the pond, we find the "Incredible Edible Todmorden" initiative in England, which has transformed public spaces into edible landscapes using compost generated from community waste. This grassroots movement has inspired many other towns to follow suit, showing that sustainable practices and local action can bear fruit - literally!

In Melbourne, Australia, the "3000acres" project has been turning underused urban spaces into vibrant community gardens fueled by locally produced compost. These vibrant green spaces are not just improving the urban landscape but are also fostering a sense of community and environmental responsibility among city dwellers.

These are only a few examples of the countless grassroots movements worldwide that are changing the face of composting. Their impact, however, extends far beyond their local neighborhoods. By every compost bin they install, every heap they turn, and every seed they plant in compost-rich soil, they are contributing to the compost revolution, impacting the whole planet.

Community Composting Initiatives

Community efforts often stand as shining examples of how collaborative action can amplify the benefits of sustainable practices. As we explore various models of community composting initiatives, we'll traverse a diversity of landscapes - from the intimate corners of neighborhood composting programs to the bustling, large-scale city-wide compost collection and distribution systems. Each model, irrespective of its scale, shines with the common goal of recycling organic waste and enriching our soils.

Let's start our exploration in Seattle, a city that has been a forerunner in city-wide composting initiatives in the United States. The city provides compost bins to residents and has made a composting yard and food waste mandatory, leading to significantly reduced landfill waste and an abundance of compost for local parks and gardens.

Next, we find ourselves in the bustling city of San Francisco, which introduced a city-wide composting program back in 2009. They provide residents with green bins for all organic waste, including food scraps and yard waste. The collected waste is then composted at a commercial facility, and the compost produced is sold to farms and vineyards.

On the East Coast, New York City's "NYC Compost Project" composting program stands out. Despite being in one of the most densely populated cities in the world, the program has succeeded in collecting food scraps from residents and converting them into compost used in local parks, gardens, and even rooftop farms.

On a smaller scale, many neighborhood composting programs are proving to be successful. For instance, the "Let Us Compost" initiative in Athens, Georgia, started by a local resident, collects food scraps from community members and delivers compost back to them while reducing the community's waste footprint.

These examples portray that community composting initiative come in all shapes and sizes, but each contributes to the more significant compost revolution. They are a testament to the power of collective action and proof that when a community comes together for a cause, change is possible and inevitable.

Challenges and Solutions in Community Composting

Starting a community composting initiative is like planting a seed – it requires nurturing, patience, and the collective efforts of a dedicated community. Yet, just like growing a plant, this endeavor comes with some manageable challenges. Let's look at some common issues that can arise and offer practical, hands-on solutions for each.

A hurdle often encountered in community composting is the logistical management of the process. Collecting the organic waste, composting it, and then distributing the final product requires a thoughtfully organized system. One possible solution is the establishment of designated collection points throughout the community. Neighbors can drop off their organic waste at these spots on specified days, helping to streamline the collection process. For the composting itself, a rotating schedule involving dedicated volunteers can keep the system running smoothly. Once the compost is ready, organize pickup days, transforming the process into a communal activity that both simplifies distribution and promotes community engagement.

Funding, naturally, is another issue that needs addressing. While the start-up costs for a composting project can vary, funds will inevitably be required. Fundraising events – think local fairs, sponsored runs, or bake sales – are a traditional but effective way to gather resources. Moreover, consider reaching out to local businesses for sponsorship or applying for environmental grants from governmental or nonprofit organizations. You could also sell the finished compost at a reasonable price, contributing to the initiative's sustainability and promoting the concept of a circular economy.

Garnering sufficient community support is another challenge that can't be overlooked. Education is key to rallying your neighbors and local businesses around the cause. Organize informational sessions and workshops that communicate the why and how of composting, highlighting the benefits for the individual and the environment. Collaborate with schools to include composting in their curriculum – this not only educates the younger generation but also ensures that the message reaches their families at home.

Keep in mind that the journey towards successful community composting, though challenging, also sparks innovation, collaboration, inspiration and fosters a greener, closely-knit neighborhood.

How to Start Your Own Community Composting Initiative

Starting your community composting initiative can be a fulfilling project. It not only helps the environment but also brings the community closer together. Here's a practical, step-by-step guide to help you kick-start your journey toward a greener neighborhood.

- Step 1: Building Awareness and Gathering Support Your first step should be to spread the word about the initiative. Use local community meetings, social media, and word-of-mouth to educate and inform your neighbors about the benefits of composting. Try to be transparent about the plans, invite questions, and welcome suggestions. It's important to create an inclusive atmosphere where everyone feels they have a stake in the initiative's success.

- Step 2: Establish a Core Team Identify and recruit enthusiastic and committed individuals willing to put in the time and effort to get the initiative off the ground. The team should ideally include individuals with different skill sets, such as project management, education and outreach, and a basic understanding of composting.

- Step 3: Securing a Composting Site You'll need a suitable location for the composting operation. Look for an accessible area with good drainage that's away from residential buildings (to avoid potential complaints about odors). You may need permission from local authorities or property owners to use the space.

- Step 4: Gathering Necessary Resources Collect necessary composting equipment like compost bins or tumblers, pitchforks, and wheelbarrows. You might consider launching a fundraising campaign to cover these costs or ask local businesses for sponsorships or donations.

- Step 5: Establishing a Collection System Set up a system for collecting organic waste from community members. You can designate collection points or organize pickup days. Ensure everyone understands what can and can't be composted to maintain the quality of the compost pile.

- Step 6: Managing the Composting Process Assign team members or volunteers to regularly turn the compost pile, monitor its temperature, and troubleshoot any issues like unpleasant smells or pests. Organizing a training session or workshop may be helpful to ensure everyone involved understands the composting process.

- Step 7: Distributing the Finished Compost Once your compost is ready (usually in 2-4 months), you need to decide how to distribute it. You could allow community members to collect it themselves or deliver it directly to local gardens or farms. Selling the compost at a reasonable price can also help fund the continued operation of the project.

This is all about creating relationships and instilling a sense of communal responsibility for our environment. So, gather your neighbors, start spreading the word, and let the compost revolution flourish.

Composting in Schools and Educational Settings

Composting in schools and educational settings helps reduce waste and encourages healthier gardens. Plus, it presents a unique opportunity to inspire the next generation about sustainability and the wonders of nature's cycles. These initiatives serve as a real-world, hands-on classroom where students learn the importance of environmental stewardship. Let's delve into the specific benefits that composting programs can bring to our schools:

- Educational Value: Composting promotes practical learning opportunities and can be integrated into diverse fields such as biology, ecology, and environmental science, among others. It provides an excellent opportunity to teach students about the cycles of nature, decomposition, and the role of organisms in the ecosystem.

- Promotes Sustainability: Implementing composting in schools raises awareness about sustainability and waste management from a young age which can have a long-lasting impact on a child's habits and attitudes toward the environment.

- Reduces Waste: As you might imagine, school cafeterias produce significant organic waste that can be composted. Instead of contributing to landfill waste, schools can turn their waste into valuable compost.

- Enriches School Gardens: Many schools have gardens where students learn to grow vegetables and flowers. The compost produced can enrich these garden soils, demonstrating a practical application of composting.

- Fosters Responsibility and Teamwork: Participating in composting programs can teach students important core values such as responsibility, teamwork, and contributing to their community.

- Engages the Wider Community: School composting programs can also engage the wider community, including parents and local residents, promoting a broader culture of sustainability.

The influence of such initiatives goes beyond the school boundaries, creating environmentally conscious citizens who can contribute significantly to sustainability and waste reduction in their communities.

After all, today's young compost enthusiasts can become tomorrow's green leaders, and that's an investment definitely worth making.

The Future of Composting: Trends, Innovations, and Opportunities

I n the grand adventure of composting, simplicity is now the key. We are witnessing a revolution where composting methods are evolving to be more approachable, practical, and user-friendly. This is terrific news for everyone, whether you're a gardening enthusiast with a sprawling backyard or an urban dweller with a small balcony filled with potted plants.

Picture this: DIY composting methods that require nothing more than your everyday kitchen scraps, a compost bin, and a small corner of your home. Sounds doable, right? These methods have opened up composting to a wider audience. The rise of these DIY techniques means that composting can be part of your lifestyle no matter how limited your resources or space is.

It's all about finding a method that suits your lifestyle and your constraints. From composting with worms (vermicomposting) to Bokashi, a method of small-scale composting using a specific group of microorganisms, composting has never been more accessible. Even apartment dwellers are finding ways to compost their food waste into rich, nutrient-filled compost for their urban gardens.

So, if you've been holding back from composting because it seemed too complicated or demanding, it's time to reconsider. Composting is simpler and more accessible than ever before.

Technology Meets Composting

Imagine a sleek, smart composter that fits neatly under your kitchen sink, silently transforming your food scraps into compost without unpleasant odors. Or picture a mobile app that guides you through composting, offering tips and reminders tailored to your specific compost setup. From compost thermometers that keep you updated on the temperature of your compost pile to moisture meters that ensure your compost has the right amount of water, technological innovations are making composting more accessible and efficient.

A standout in this field of innovation is the rise of electric composters. Designed for indoor use, these gadgets accelerate the composting process and handle the decomposition of your food waste for you. All you need to do is add your kitchen scraps, and the composter takes care of the rest. In just a few weeks, you'll have ready-to-use compost.

Another fascinating development is the growth of composting apps. These handy tools help you track your compost's progress, send you reminders about when to turn your compost pile, and even offer troubleshooting tips for any issues that might come up.

But perhaps one of the most fun innovations in this field is using virtual reality (VR) and augmented reality (AR) to educate people about composting. These interactive experiences provide a hands-on approach to learning about composting, immersing you in the process and making learning about composting an exciting adventure.

Local communities have an enormous role to play in the future of composting, and an exciting trend we're seeing is the growing number of local councils, municipalities, and organizations that are throwing their support behind composting.

Let's say you've just started composting and are faced with a challenge you don't know how to handle. What if I tell you that having access to a local composting support line or a composting expert who can guide you through the issue is possible? This isn't some far-off dream; this is a reality in many places where local authorities and organizations have recognized the value of composting and are investing in providing resources and support for individuals and households embarking on their composting journey.

Incentives and Support for Composting

Many municipalities are introducing incentives to promote composting. These incentives range from subsidies for composting bins or tools to discounts on property taxes for individuals who compost. Some places even offer free composting workshops or courses to educate the public about the benefits and process of composting.

There's also the rise of composting grants. Several councils and organizations offer grants to individuals, schools, and community groups who like to start a composting project. This financial support can go a long way in helping kickstart composting initiatives and encouraging more people to compost.

Local support is becoming a major driving force in the world of composting, making it easier and more appealing for anyone to start their composting journey. So, if you're considering composting, check out the resources and support available in your local community. You might be pleasantly surprised by the help and incentives available! The future of composting looks brighter with such robust community support.

The Role of Composting in Climate Change Mitigation

There's a wave of environmental awareness sweeping across the globe as more people become conscious of the critical issues we're facing, like climate change, pollution, and waste management. Amidst this backdrop, composting is emerging as a surprisingly powerful tool in the fight against these challenges.

Let's step back for a moment and imagine your kitchen scraps. You know, the peelings, the coffee grounds, the old leftovers you didn't quite get around to finishing. Now think about what happens to those scraps. If you're like many people, they probably go straight into the trash can, and from there, they end up in the landfill.

But what if we could change that narrative? This is where composting comes in. By composting your kitchen scraps, you are effectively diverting waste from the landfill.

But that's just the start. In the landfill, organic waste breaks down anaerobically (without oxygen) and releases methane, a potent greenhouse gas contributing to climate change. Composting, on the other hand, is an aerobic process (it requires oxygen) and produces far less methane.

So, by composting, you are reducing the volume of waste and helping to lower greenhouse gas emissions.

But the story gets even better. Healthy soils have improved structure and water-holding capacity, reducing erosion and runoff. Compost, rich in organic matter, enhances soil health. They also store more carbon, serving as a "sink" that locks away carbon dioxide and mitigates climate change.

Home composting might seem like a small action, but its potential impact is huge. It's an empowering way for individuals to play a direct role in tackling environmental issues. Composting transforms waste into a resource, turning a problem into a solution.

The Future is Green - Upcoming Trends in Composting

As we stand on the brink of a new age in composting, it's exhilarating to imagine what the future holds for enthusiasts of this timeless practice. The trends we see today are a testament to the creativity and innovation individuals and communities worldwide are applying to this age-old method of recycling organic material. Let's explore a few of these exciting, emerging trends in the world of composting:

1. Community Composting: This trend is gaining momentum as more people realize the benefits of pooling resources to create shared compost piles or facilities. These community composting programs help streamline the composting process and make it more accessible for those who may not have the space or resources to compost individually.

2. Composting in Schools: Schools are increasingly integrating composting into their curriculum as a hands-on, practical way to teach students about sustainability and waste management. This trend is promising for its

immediate benefits (like reducing waste and creating compost for school gardens) and because it's shaping the next generation of environmentally conscious citizens.

3. Urban Farming and Composting: As urban farming grows in popularity, so does the use of compost within the city limits. Rooftop gardens, vertical farms, and community gardens in city parks are all places where composting plays a crucial role. By using compost, these urban farms can create rich, fertile soil even in the most concrete-heavy environments, contributing to local food production and enhancing city life.

4. Technology-aided Composting: There's a surge in composting gadgets and technologies designed to make composting more efficient. From smart compost bins that monitor temperature and moisture levels to mobile apps that guide you through the composting process, technology is making composting more accessible and enjoyable for everyone.

5. Composting Policy and Legislation: In some parts of the world, composting is becoming more than just an environmentally friendly practice—it's becoming a legal requirement. Some cities and countries are introducing legislation that encourages or mandates composting, which will noticeably impact the future of composting.

These emerging trends all point to a future where composting is widespread, integrated into daily life and recognized for its crucial role in building sustainable communities.

Frequently Asked Questions (FAQs) on Composting

Whether you're a bright-eyed beginner ready to set up your first compost pile or a seasoned veteran with a well-turned heap, the path of a composter is one of continual learning. In this chapter, we aim to clear any confusion, simplify the process, and provide you with the understanding you need for successful composting. Let's move forward and respond to these questions, making your path to composting mastery smoother and boosting your confidence throughout the process.

Q1: Can I compost at home if I live in an apartment?

Answer: Absolutely, yes! While you might not have the luxury of a backyard, there are still plenty of ways to compost in an apartment setting. One popular method is vermicomposting, which uses worms to break down food scraps into nutrient-rich compost. You can easily keep a small vermicomposting bin under your sink or on your balcony. There are also countertop compost bins and electric composters designed specifically for indoor use. These compact systems can be an efficient and odor-free way to compost your kitchen scraps.

Q2: What can I compost, and what should I avoid composting?

Answer: You can compost various organic materials, including fruit and vegetable scraps, coffee grounds, tea bags, eggshells, leaves, grass clippings, and small amounts of shredded paper or cardboard. However, there are some things you should avoid composting. This includes meat, dairy, and oily foods, which can attract pests and cause unpleasant odors. Additionally, diseased plants, pet waste, and weed seeds are best left out of your compost pile to avoid spreading disease or weeds in your garden.

Q3: How long does it take to make compost?

Answer: The composting process can vary significantly in length depending on several factors. These include the materials you're composting, the size of your compost pile, the temperature, and how often you turn the pile. In general, compost can be ready anywhere from two months to a year. Composting is a natural process, and patience is key!

Q4: My compost pile is smelly. What am I doing wrong?

Answer: Compost should have a fresh, earthy smell. If it's producing a strong, unpleasant odor, it could mean there's an imbalance in your compost pile. The smell could be caused by too many green materials (like kitchen scraps) and not enough brown materials (like leaves or straw) to balance it out. Try adding more brown materials to the pile. Another reason could be poor aeration, which might require turning the pile more frequently to get oxygen into it.

Q5: How can I use my finished compost?

Answer: Finished compost is a versatile addition to your garden. You can mix it into garden soil to improve its fertility and structure or use it as mulch around plants to suppress weeds and retain moisture. It's also great for potting mixes or as a lawn top dressing. Compost is the ultimate soil conditioner, providing a range of nutrients and enhancing the soil's ability to hold onto water and nutrients.

Q6: What's the difference between composting and vermicomposting?

Answer: While both processes recycle organic waste into nutrient-rich compost, they do so in different ways. Traditional composting relies on naturally occurring bacteria and fungi to decompose the material, often facilitated by manually turning the compost pile. Vermicomposting, on the other hand, uses worms (specifically, red wrigglers) to consume and excrete the organic material, turning it into a fine, nutrient-rich compost known as worm castings. Vermicomposting is typically faster than traditional composting and can be done on a smaller scale, making it a popular choice for indoor or urban composting.

Q7: Can I compost dairy and meat products?

Answer: Generally, it's not recommended to compost dairy and meat products at home. They can attract pests like rats and raccoons and may also create unpleasant odors as they decompose. However, some more advanced composting methods and systems, like Bokashi or hot composting, can handle these types of waste. These methods require specific conditions and more effort to manage, so they're not typically recommended for beginners.

Q8: Why does my compost pile have a bad odor?

Answer: A healthy compost pile should have a pleasant, earthy smell. If your compost pile is giving off a foul odor, it's usually a sign that something is off balance. One common issue is too much moisture - this can cause the compost pile to become anaerobic or oxygen-starved, producing smelly gases. To remedy this, try turning the pile to let it dry out a bit and add more 'browns' - dry, carbon-rich materials like leaves, straw, or newspaper - to help soak up excess moisture. It could also be that there are too many 'greens' or nitrogen-rich materials, such as vegetable scraps or grass clippings, causing an excess of nitrogen, which can also cause bad smells. Add more 'browns' to bring the pile back into balance

Q9: What should I do if my compost pile is attracting pests?

Answer: Attracting pests is often a sign that you might be composting inappropriate items. Meat, dairy, and cooked foods can attract animals, so avoid composting these if pests are a problem. Another solution is to ensure that your compost pile is well-covered, which can help to deter pests. Regularly turning your compost can also discourage animals from settling in your pile.

Q10: How can I speed up the composting process?

Answer: Composting is a natural process that can take anywhere from a couple of months to a year, depending on various factors. However, you can do a few things to speed it up. First, turn your compost pile regularly, about once a week or when it starts to heat up, to aerate it and provide oxygen to the microbes that are hard at work breaking down your compost materials. Second, maintain a good balance of 'greens' (nitrogen-rich materials like food scraps and fresh grass clippings) and 'browns' (carbon-rich materials like leaves, straw, and paper). A ratio of about 2:1 browns to greens is often recommended. Third, make sure your compost pile is moist but not waterlogged. The moisture level should be similar to a wrung-out sponge.

Q11: Is there a specific ratio of greens and browns I should maintain in my compost pile?

Answer: A good rule of thumb is to aim for a ratio of about three parts browns to 1 part greens by volume. 'Browns' are carbon-rich materials like leaves, straw, and paper, and they help add bulk and facilitate air circulation in your compost pile. 'Greens' are nitrogen-rich materials like vegetable scraps, coffee grounds, and fresh grass clippings, and they provide the nitrogen needed by composting microbes. If your pile is smelly or seems to be composting very slowly, adjusting the ratio of greens and browns can often help.

Q12: Can I compost in the winter?

Answer: Yes, composting in winter is doable, but expect the process to slow down due to cold temperatures. Yet, you can still add materials to your compost pile all winter. It might take longer for things to break down compared to warmer weather but don't worry; once spring comes around with its warmer weather, your winter compost will quickly turn into rich food for your garden or houseplants.

CONCLUSION

And there you have it – we've turned over every leaf, quite literally, in this comprehensive journey into the world of composting.

Beginning with the essentials of composting, we've dug deep into the scientific principles that underpin this transformative process. Together, we've explored different composting methods, unearthing each method's benefits and potential challenges. Our journey then took us through the fascinating world of soil health and the role composting plays in creating rich, fertile soil fit for the healthiest plants.

You've been introduced to the broader scope of sustainable living and how composting snugly fits into this picture. We examined how composting extends beyond our backyards and into our communities, where collective efforts amplify the benefits manifold. The critical role of advocacy and grassroots movements in spreading the compost revolution was another cornerstone of our exploration.

Through this journey, we've navigated the exciting future of composting with emerging trends, innovations, and opportunities that lie in wait. To equip you further, we answered some of the most frequently asked questions in the world of composting.

If there's one key takeaway, let it be this: composting is truly a journey. There will be trials, errors, lessons, and successes. The joy lies in participating in a process that deeply connects us with the cycle of life and nature.

By opening this book and reading until the end, you've demonstrated not just curiosity but a commitment – a commitment toward a greener, more sustainable future. Every scoop of kitchen waste you divert from the trashcan to the compost bin is a step toward reducing your carbon footprint. Each time you enrich your soil with compost, you're contributing to a more biodiverse, resilient ecosystem. These actions might seem small, but collectively, they're monumental.

Thank you for embarking on this journey. Your commitment to learning about composting, your readiness to adapt your lifestyle, and your desire to contribute positively to the environment are commendable. Remember, every compost pile or worm bin is a badge of honor – a symbol of your personal commitment to sustainability. Wear it proudly.

As we close this book, it's not the end of your composting journey, but rather, the beginning. Composting isn't a one-time task but a lifelong commitment to sustainability, a testament to our capacity as humans to live in harmony with nature.

Thank you for your time, commitment, and contribution to a healthier planet. Let's continue to grow, learn, and compost. After all, the future of our planet starts in our backyards. Here's to you and your composting journey – a lifelong commitment to sustainability.

Lastly, we can call composting a lifestyle; adopt it as yours!

References

In this section, I have compiled a list of valuable sources and references that have contributed to the understanding and knowledge about composting presented in this book.

•⬚Martin D., & Gershuny G. (1992). The Rodale Book of Composting: Easy Methods for Every Gardener. Rodale Books.

•⬚Campbell S. (1998). Let It Rot!: The Gardener's Guide to Composting. Storey Publishing.

•⬚Lanza P. (1998). Lasagna Gardening: A New Layering System for Bountiful Gardens. Rodale Books.

•⬚Nancarrow L., & Taylor J. (1998). The Worm Book: The Complete Guide to Gardening and Composting with Worms, Ten Speed Press

•⬚Jenkins J. (2005). Humanure Handbook: A Guide to Composting Human Manure. J. Jenkins Ink

•⬚Bradley F.M., Ellis B., Martin D. (2010). The Organic Gardener's Handbook of Natural Pest and Disease Control. Rodale Books.

•⬚Flowerdew B., (2012). Composting: Bob's Basics, Skyhorse Pub Co.

•⬚Hemenway, T. (2013). Gaia's Garden: A Guide to Home-Scale Permaculture. Chelsea Green Publishing.

•□Gilbert J., (2015). The Composting Troubleshooter: How to Compost and What to Do If It Goes Wrong, Carbon Clarity

•□Balz M. & Stockton A., (2017). Composting for a New Generation: Latest Techniques for the Bin and Beyond, Cool Springs Press

•□Appelhof M., & Olszewski J. (2017). Worms Eat My Garbage: How to Set Up and Maintain a Worm Composting System. Storey Publishing.

•□Solomon S., (2021). Organic Gardener's Composting, Aeterna

•□David The Good, (2021). Compost Everything: The Good Guide to Extreme Composting, Good Books

•□Balz M., (2021). No-Waste Composting: Small-Space Waste Recycling, Indoors and Out, Cool Springs Press

Articles

•□Aaron Sidder (2016), The Green, Brown, and Beautiful Story of Compost – retrieved from https://www.nationalgeographic.com/culture/article/compost--a-history-in-green-and-brown

•□Rachel Ross (2018), The Science Behind Composting – retrieved from https://www.livescience.com/63559-composting.html

•□Shelia Hu (2020), Composting 101 - retrieved from https://www.nrdc.org/stories/composting-101

•□EPA (2023), Reducing the Impact of Wasted Food by Feeding the Soil and Composting - retrieved from https://www.epa.gov/sustainable-management-food/reducing-impact-wasted-food-feeding-soil-and-composting

•□Michael J. Coren (2023), Why composting doesn't have to be hard anymore - retrieved from https://www.washingtonpost.com/climate-environment/2023/02/21/home-composting-new-technology/

About the Author

Raised amidst the wholesome earthiness of farmland and bathed in his father's wisdom, a seasoned farmer, Oliver Thorne's romance with gardening was nurtured from an early age. His fascination for the cycles of nature, the richness of the soil, and the beauty of growth soon became more than just a hobby - it transformed into a profound passion and a lifelong pursuit. Continuing his father's legacy and equipped with an insatiable thirst for knowledge, Oliver dived deep into horticulture, permaculture, and sustainable living. He extended his horizons and turned his hands-on experience into formal studies, further enriching his knowledge and understanding of the beautiful and intricate world of plants and soil.

Today, Oliver is a dedicated gardener, enthusiastic educator, and tireless innovator. His writing, which beautifully amalgamates his rich experience with rigorous research, has become a beacon for beginners and experienced gardeners alike. His workshops, fueled by his infectious passion, impart knowledge and inspire deep respect and love for the environment.

Always at the cutting edge of composting techniques, Oliver continues to explore and innovate, tirelessly experimenting with new ways to turn waste into gold. He shares his expertise and discoveries through his books and articles, inviting you to join him in embracing a greener lifestyle and experiencing the joy of turning your garden into a fertile haven.

www.ingramcontent.com/pod-product-compliance
Lightning Source LLC
Chambersburg PA
CBHW070921120626
46546CB00001B/351